THE COMMON LAW LIBRARY

SALE OF GOODS

OTHER VOLUMES IN THE COMMON LAW LIBRARY

Chitty on Contracts
Clerk & Lindsell on Torts
Chitty & Jacob's Queen's Bench Forms
Bullen & Leake & Jacob's Precedents of Pleadings
Charlesworth and Percy on Negligence
Bowstead & Reynolds on Agency
Gatley on Libel and Slander
McGregor on Damages
Phipson on Evidence
Jackson & Powell on Professional Negligence
Goff & Jones, The Law of Restitution
Arlidge, Eady & Smith on Contempt

THE COMMON LAW LIBRARY

BENJAMIN'S
SALE OF GOODS

FIRST SUPPLEMENT

TO THE

EIGHTH EDITION

Up-to-date to June 2012

SWEET & MAXWELL

 THOMSON REUTERS

BENJAMIN'S TREATISE ON THE LAW OF SALE OF PERSONAL PROPERTY WITH REFERENCES TO THE FRENCH CODE AND CIVIL LAW

First Edition	(1868)	Judah Philip Benjamin
Second Edition	(1873)	” ” ”
Third Edition	(1883)	A. B. Pearson and H. F. Boyd
Fourth Edition	(1888)	A. B. Pearson-Gee and H. F. Boyd
Fifth Edition	(1906)	W. C. A. Ker and A. R. Butterworth
Sixth Edition	(1920)	W. C. A. Ker
Seventh Edition	(1931)	His Hon. Judge A. R. Kennedy, K.C.
Eighth Edition	(1950)	The Hon. Sir Donald Leslie Finnemore and Arthur E. James

BENJAMIN'S SALE OF GOODS

First Edition	(1974)	General Editor A. G. Guest
Second Edition	(1981)	” ” ”
Third Edition	(1987)	” ” ”
Fourth Edition	(1992)	” ” ”
Fifth Edition	(1997)	” ” ”
Sixth Edition	(2002)	” ” ”
Seventh Edition	(2006)	” ” ”
Eighth Edition	(2010)	General Editor M. Bridge

Published in 2012 by Thomson Reuters (Legal) Limited
(Registered in England & Wales, Company No.1679046.
Registered Office and address for service:
100 Avenue Road, London NW3 3PF)
trading as Sweet & Maxwell.

Typeset by LBJ Typesetting of Kingsclere.
Printed and bound by CPI Group (UK) Ltd, Croydon, CR0 4YY.

For further information on our products and services, visit
www.sweetandmaxwell.co.uk.

A CIP catalogue record for this book is available from
the British Library

ISBN-978-0-414-02291-1

HOW TO USE THIS SUPPLEMENT

This is the First Supplement to the Eighth Edition of *Benjamin's Sale of Goods* and has been compiled according to the structure of the main work.

At the beginning of each chapter of this supplement the mini table of contents from the main volume has been included. Where a heading in this table of contents has been marked with the symbol ■, the material under that heading has been added to or amended in this supplement.

Within each chapter, updating information is referenced to the relevant paragraph in the main volume.

CONTENTS

Part One

NATURE AND FORMATION OF THE CONTRACT OF SALE

Part Two

PROPERTY AND RISK

Part Three

PERFORMANCE OF THE CONTRACT

CONTENTS

Part Four

DEFECTIVE GOODS

Part Five

CONSUMER PROTECTION

Part Six

REMEDIES

Part Seven

OVERSEAS SALES

Part Eight

CONFLICT OF LAWS

PREFACE

This is the first Supplement to the 8th edition of *Benjamin's Sale of Goods*. Since that edition appeared in 2010, there has been a substantial amount of case law affecting most of the chapters in this book, as well as a significant amount of change in the secondary legislation dealing with consumer transactions in Chapter 14, where particular account should be taken of Directive 2011/83/EU on consumer rights. Some further consolidating material has been added to the chapters on letters of credit and autonomous guarantees (Chapters 23–24), continuing the recasting of the material on these subjects that was substantially done in the 8th edition. In Chapter 26, dealing with the conflict of laws, and in a new Appendix, contained in this Supplement, a summary account has been given of a draft Common European Sales Law which, if adopted, will take the form of an EC Regulation. The Common European Sales Law, heavily influenced by the Vienna Convention on the International Sale of Goods and further supplemented by the civil law tradition, is designed to provide contracting parties with a transnational law that they might opt into in preference to existing national law. It is designed for consumer transactions and for only those commercial transactions where one of the parties is a small to medium enterprise.

Of the case law that has appeared, particular account may at this point be taken of the following. In the area of contractual formation and content, *GHSP Inc v AB Electronic Ltd* [2011] 1 Lloyd's Rep. 432 deals with the battle of forms and *Springwell Navigation Corp v JP Morgan Chase Bank* [2010] EWCA 1221 with entire agreement clauses.

In *Société Générale SA v Saad Trading* [2011] EWHC 2424 (Comm), the court deals with the presentation of documents by the beneficiary of a letter of credit and the forwarding of those documents by a nominated bank. The refusal of documents is engaged by *Fortis Bank SA/NV v Indian Overseas Bank (Nos 1 & 2)* [2011] EWCA Civ 58.

On the Judgments Regulation, there is *Pammer v Reederei Karl Schlüter GmbH & Co KG* [2011] 2 All E.R. (Comm) 888, concerning internet activity, and *Electrosteel Europe SA v Edil Centro SpA* [2011] I.L. Pr. 28, on the place of delivery. The subject of international supply contracts and exclusion from the provisions of the Unfair Contract Terms Act 1977 comes up in *Air Transworld Ltd v Bombardier Inc* [2012] EWHC 243 (Comm), and *Kingspan Environmental Ltd v Borealis A/S* [2012] EWHC 1147 (Comm) deals with an attempt to contract out of the Unfair Contract Terms Act 1977 by means of a choice of law clause.

In the area of remedies, there have been noteworthy decisions on the recovery of money on a failure of consideration (*Giedo van der Garde BV v Force India Formula One Team* [2010] EWHC 2373 (QB)), on recoverability of expenses incurred on hedging transactions as a cost of taking mitigating action (*Choil Trading SA v Sahara Energy Resources Ltd* [2010] EWHC 374 (Comm)), and on the assumption of responsibility for loss and the extent of recoverable damages

(*Sylvia Shipping Co Ltd v Progress Bulk Carriers Ltd (The Sylvia)* [2010] EWHC 542 (Comm)). The difficulties introduced by Part 5A of the Sale of Goods Act, so far as the legislation concerns the cost of replacing consumer goods, are addressed by *Gebr Weber GmbH v Wittmer* [2011] 3 C.M.L.R. 27.

Samarenko v Dawn Hill House Ltd [2011] EWCA Civ 1445 is an important decision on timely performance and making time of the essence, and *KG Bominflot Bunkergesellschaft fur Mineraloele mbH & Co AG v Petroplus Marketing AG (The Mercini Lady)* [2010] EWCA Civ 1145, which appears in more than one place in this Supplement, is an important decision on transit, quality and risk. On proprietary matters, *Wincanton Group Ltd v Garbe Logistics UK 1 SARL* [2011] EWHC 905 (Ch) deals with the passing of property and *Great Elephant Corp v Trafigura Beheer BV* [2012] EWHC 1745 (Comm) provides guidance on the effect of third party interference with goods in respect of the seller's right to sell and the buyer's right to quiet possession in s.12 of the Sale of Goods Act.

Numerous developments have arisen in the area of export sales. Particular notice should be taken of *Carewins Development (China) Ltd v Bright Fortune Shipping Ltd* [2009] 1 HKLRD 429 (on the production of straight bills of lading), *The Dolphina* [2011] SGHC 273 (on spent bills of lading), *A P Moeller-Maersk A/S v Sonaec Villas Cen Sad Fadoul* [2010] EWHC 355 (Comm) (on the Carriage of Goods by Sea Act 1992), *Glencore Energy (UK) Ltd v Sonol Israel Ltd (The Team Anmaj)* [2011] EWHC 2756 (Comm) (on demurrage provisions in sale contracts) and *Thai Marparn Trading Co Ltd v Louis Dreyfus Commodities Asia Pte Ltd* [2011] EWHC 2494 (Comm) (on notice of expected readiness to load and shipment periods).

Mention should also be made of the decision of the Supreme Court in *ENE Kos v Petroleo Brasileiro SA (The Kos)* [2012] UKSC 17 (on non-contractual bailment).

Professor M.G. Bridge
London

TABLE OF CASES

TABLE OF UNITED KINGDOM STATUTES

TABLE OF UNITED KINGDOM STATUTORY INSTRUMENTS

TABLE OF EUROPEAN LEGISLATION

TABLE OF INTERNATIONAL CONVENTIONS

TABLE OF FOREIGN LEGISLATION

Canada

Note: All references in the Main Work to Treitel, *The Law of Contract* (12th edn, edited by Peel), are replaced by Treitel, *The Law of Contract* (13th edn, 2011). All references to *Carver on Bills of Lading* (2nd edn, 2005), are replaced by *Carver on Bills of Lading* (3rd edn, 2011). All references to *Clerk and Lindsell on Torts* (19th edn) are replaced by *Clerk and Lindsell on Torts* (20th edn). All references to Goff and Jones, *The Law of Restitution* (7th edn), are replaced by Goff and Jones, *The Law of Unjust Enrichment* (8th edn, 2011). Some paragraph references have been updated in this Supplement.

Part One

NATURE AND FORMATION OF THE CONTRACT OF SALE

CHAPTER 1

THE CONTRACT OF SALE OF GOODS

1. THE SALE OF GOODS ACTS

The Sale of Goods Act 1979

[*Add at the end of fn.9*]   **1–001**
Bankruptcy and Diligence etc. (Scotland) Act 2007, ss.226(1), 227, Sch.6 Pt.1 (with s.223); SSI 2008/11 art.3, Sch.2 (with art.9) repealed part of s.62(5).

[*Amend fn.12*]
Macleod, *Consumer Sales Law* (2009)

Application of Code to modern conditions

[*Add at the end of fn.25*]   **1–003**
See *BSS Group Plc v Makers (UK) Ltd (t/a Allied Services)* [2011] EWCA Civ 809 at [6].

Construction of consolidating statute

[*Add at the end of fn.29*]   **1–004**
Where a provision in a consolidating statute is ambiguous or obscure, the court may be able to apply the rule in *Pepper v Hart* [1993] A.C. 593 (see below,

para.1–005 at fn.35) and refer to parliamentary materials relating to the statute: *Johnson (Inspector of Taxes) v The Prudential Assurance Co Ltd* [1996] STC 647.

The Act and equity

1–008   *[Amend fn.58]*
Treitel, *The Law of Contract* (13th edn, 2011), pp.913–914.

[Add at the end of fn.61]
An equivalent provision in Canada has been held to include the rules of equity: Sale of Goods Act, RSA 2000, c.S-2, s.58(1); *Wilson v Airdrie Auto & RV Sales Ltd* 2010 ABPC 96 at [10] (Alberta).

1–009   *[Amend fn.65]*
Treitel, *The Law of Contract* (13th edn, 2011), pp.913–914.

2.   RELATED STATUTES

Bills of Sale Acts

1–016   *[Add at the end of fn.102]*
The government acknowledged that consumer complaints about loans secured against bills of sale were increasing (*e.g. Welcome Financial Services Ltd v Nine Regions Ltd (t/a Log Book Loans)* [2010] 2 Lloyd's Rep. 426); but decided against regulation and instead placed its faith in a voluntary code of practice: BIS, *Government Response to the Consultation on Proposals to Ban the Use of Bills of Sale for Consumer Lending* (2011); Consumer Credit Trade Association, *Code of Practice: Bills of Sale for Lending Regulated under the Consumer Credit Act: A Commitment to Responsible Lending* (2011); Sheehan, 126 L.Q.R. 356 (2010); McBain, 5 J.B.L. 475 (2011).

[Add at the end of fn.105]
This may include after-acquired property: *Chapman (t/a Chapman & Co Solicitors) v Wilson* [2010] EWHC 1746 (Ch).

EC legislation

1–023   *[Amend title to]*

European legislation

[Add new fn.174A at the end of the paragraph on p.24]

[174A] The Directive on Consumer Rights (2011/83/EU), which must be implemented by the end of 2013, replaces or amends directives on distance contracts (97/7/EC), contracts negotiated away from business premises (85/577/EEC), unfair terms (93/13/EEC) and consumer sales and guarantees (1999/44/EC). This has prompted the UK government to propose a new "Consumer Bill of Rights", which will update and clarify the law on consumer sales of goods, services and digital content, repealing and replacing various existing regulations and repealing or amending parts of the Misrepresentation Act 1967, the Supply of Goods (Implied Terms) Act 1973, the Unfair Contract Terms Act 1977, the Sale of Goods Act 1979, the Sale and Supply of Goods and Services Act 1994 in so far as they deal with consumer sales. See B.E.R.R., *Consumer Law Review* (2008) and *A Better Deal for Consumers* (2009); B.I.S., press release (September 18, 2011, available at *http://nds.coi.gov.uk/content/Detail.aspx?ReleaseID=421254&NewsAreaID=2*). More radically, the Commission has proposed the Common European Sales Law, which would exist alongside national sales laws and apply if both parties to a cross-border contract (whether business–business or consumer–business) adopted it and one of the parties was established in the EU. This idea has not been well received by the UK government. See Hesselink, 20 E.R.P.L. 195 (2012); McMeel, 27 B.J.I.B. & F.L. 3 (2012); Monaghan, 33 Comp. Law 111 (2012).

The Uniform Laws on International Sales, and the Vienna Convention on Contracts for the International Sale of Goods

[*Add at the end of fn.177*]   **1–024**
Other major trading countries that have not ratified the Convention are Brazil, India, South Africa and Taiwan. Brazil is in the process of incorporating the Convention into national law.

[*Add at the end of fn.181*]
Statutory requirements regarding signatures may be satisfied in an electronic communication if the signatory's conduct indicates "an authenticating intention to a reasonable person": *J Pereira Fernandes SA v Mehta* [2006] 1 W.L.R. 1543 at [1552] (Statute of Frauds 1688 s.4).

3.   THE CONTRACT OF SALE

(b) *Contract of Sale Distinguished from Other Transactions*

Sale distinguished from contract for work and materials

[*Add at the end of fn.270*]   **1–041**
Wincanton Group Ltd v Garbe Logistics UK 1 SARL [2011] EWHC 905 (Ch).

Sale distinguished from contract of agency

[*Insert new fn.316A after the sub-heading on p.43*]   **1–048**

316A *McCandless Aircraft LC v Payne* [2010] EWHC 1835 (QB) at [4].

Transactions involving persons subject to incapacity

[*Amend fn.495*]   **1–076**

Treitel, *The Law of Contract* (13th edn, 2011), pp.585–586. But see Goff and Jones, *The Law of Unjust Enrichment* (8th edn, 2011), paras 24–10—24–27, 34–11.

4. SUBJECT MATTER OF THE CONTRACT

(a) *Goods*

Computer software

1–086   [*Add at the end of fn.578*]
In *Southwark LBC v IBM UK Ltd* [2011] EWHC 549 (TCC) at [97], Aikenhead J. expressed the view, *obiter*, that a disc impressed with software constitutes goods under the Act.

Human remains and parts of the body

1–089   [*Add at the end of fn.614*]
Harmon and Laurie, 69 C.L.J. 476 (2010).

Goods and land under the modern statutes

1–092   [*Add at the end of fn.633*]
This issue is not dealt with in the Law Commission's report, *Making Land Work: Easements, Covenants and Profits à Prendre* (2011).

Buildings

1–096   [*Insert into fn.678 after the reference to* Chelsea Yacht & Boat *case*]
and *Mew v Tristmire Ltd* [2012] 1 W.L.R. 852 (a houseboat on a platform did not have sufficient permanence to make it part of the plot on which the platform stood)

[*Add at the end of fn.681*]
Somme Limited v Central House Movers Limited HC Wanganui CIV-2011-483-2 [2011] NZHC 1007 (relocatable house); *Robert & Webster v Herbert* 2011 BCPC 275 (BC, Canada) (movable building); but see *Con-Tech Systems Ltd v 2044692 Ontario Inc* 2010 ONSC 1719 (Ontario) (manufacturing facility not goods).

(b) *Classes of Goods*

Agreement to pay differences distinguished

1–104   [*Amend fn.729*]

Gambling Act 2005 ss.334(1)(c), 356(3)(d), (4), (5), Sch.17. The Financial Services and Markets Act 2000 s.412 is rendered redundant by s.334(1)(e) of the 2005 Act.

Specific goods

[Line 6, insert new fn.760A after "substitution"]   **1–114**

760A Cited in *Aercap Partners 1 Ltd v Aviva Asset Management AB* [2010] EWHC 2431 (Comm) at [56].

Ascertained goods

[Add at the end of fn.780]   **1–118**
Astrazeneca UK Ltd v Albermarle International Corp [2011] 2 C.L.C. 252 at [304].

CHAPTER 2

FORMATION OF THE CONTRACT

[*Amend fn.1*]
Lloyd, *Information Technology Law* (6th edn).

1. AGREEMENT

Offer distinguished from invitation to treat

2–002   [*Amend fn.7*]
Treitel, *The Law of Contract* (13th edn, 2011), pp.11–16.

[*Add at the end of fn.14*]
Merton London Borough Council v Sinclair Collis Ltd [2011] 1 W.L.R. 570 (sale of goods does not require face-to-face dealing and can be achieved through vending machine).

[*Add at the end of fn.16*]
On "click-wrap" contracts see *Ryanair Ltd v Billigfluege.de GmbH* [2010] IEHC 47; Macdonald 19 I.J.L. & I.T. 285 (2011).

[*Amend fn.20*]
Treitel, *The Law of Contract* (13th edn, 2011), p.14.

Tenders

2–003   [*Add at the end of the text*]
While English judges have made only limited use of the *Blackpool and Fylde Aero Club* case, courts in Australia, Canada and New Zealand have been more willing to conclude that public tendering is subject to a process contract, which requires the awarding body to observe the form and conditions in the invitation to tender. There was a breach where, in spite of a statement in the invitation to tender that the contract would go to the lowest conforming tender, the award was made to a bidder who did not conform (*Pratt Contractors Ltd v Palmerston North City Council* [1995] 1 N.Z.L.R. 469). In *Hughes Aircraft Systems International v Airservices Australia* (1997) 146 A.L.R. 1, the court held there was an implied

term in the tender process contract that the authority would evaluate the tenders fairly and would give all conforming bidders an equal opportunity. The case law is most developed in Canada, following *The Queen v Ron Engineering & Construction Eastern Ltd* (1981) 119 D.L.R. (3d) 267. See Percy, 28 Const. L.J. 106 (2012).

Sales by auction

[*Add at the end of fn.29*]   2–004
The auctioneer may be negligent in advising an auction estimate that no reasonable valuer would have placed on the item: *Coleridge v Sotheby's* [2012] EWHC 370 (Ch).

[*Add at the end of fn.37*]
A reverse auction does not seem to constitute a sale. The winning bid is the lowest unique bid at the end of a stipulated time. The auctioneer's earnings come from the price paid by the winning bidder and the fee paid by bidders for each bid made. Such an "auction" is probably a lottery, which is regulated under the Gambling Act 2005, or, if skill, knowledge or judgement are required, a prize competition, which is not regulated.

Acceptance

[*Add at the end of fn.53*]   2–011
For a critique of these cases, see Mik, 19 I.J.L. & I.T. 324 (2011).

Incorporation of standard or printed terms

[*Add at the end of fn.70*]   2–012
Another form is the "browse-wrap" where the website visitor does not indicate agreement to contract by clicking: *Van Tassell v United Marketing Group LLC* 795 F.Supp.2d 770 (N.D.Ill, 2007); Macdonald 19 I.J.L. & I.T. 285 (2011). Generally, Mik, 19 I.J.L. & I.T. 324 (2011).

[*Add at the end of fn.73*]
See also, *Van Tassell v United Marketing Group LLC* 795 F.Supp.2d 770 (N.D.Ill, 2007).

The "Battle of forms"

[*Add at the end of fn.77*]   2–013
In *GHSP Inc v AB Electronic Ltd* [2011] 1 Lloyd's Rep. 432, the court summarised the main principles: the test as to the terms of the contract is objective, subject to taking into account the factual matrix; the ordinary principles of offer and acceptance, certainty and sufficiency of terms apply; normally, the contract is formed on those terms that were received without objection from the recipient; conduct will only indicate acceptance of the terms where, on an objective view, there is an intention to accept; where, as in this case, there was no agreed intention to use either set of terms, the contract (if any) must be based on other terms (here the terms implied by the Sale of Goods Act 1979). See also, *Trebor Bassett Holdings Ltd v ADT Fire and Security Plc* [2011] EWHC 1936 (TCC).

Unsolicited goods

2–014   [*Add at the end of fn.81*]
See also Austen-Baker, 35 C.L.W.R. 247 (2006).

3.   PARTIES

Capacity of parties

2–028   [*Amend fn.164*]
This view is rejected in Goff and Jones, *The Law of Unjust Enrichment* (8th edn, 2011), para.24–20.

Contractual capacity of minors

2–029   [*Amend fn.168*]
Treitel, *The Law of Contract* (13th edn, 2011), pp.566–586.

Executory contracts for necessaries

2–033   [*Amend fn.210*]
Treitel, *The Law of Contract* (13th edn, 2011), pp.569–570. Goff and Jones, *The Law of Unjust Enrichment* (8th edn, 2011), para.24–16.

4.   THE PRICE

[*Amend heading on p.138, delete* **2–243** *and insert* **2–043**]

Price must be in money

2–044   [*Add at the end of fn.265*]
Where the payment made by the buyer to the seller is intended to cover the latter's tax liability under the sale, this will not form part of the price under the sale contract: *cf. Chalabi v Agha-Jaffar* [2011] EWCA Civ 1535 (share purchase).

Failure of valuation

2–051   [*Add at the end of fn.304*]
In general, valuations provided by experts may only be challenged where there has been a "manifest error", that is, "oversights or blunders so obvious and obviously capable of affecting the determination as to admit of no difference of opinion": *Veba Oil Supply & Trading GmbH v Petrotrade Inc* [2001] EWCA Civ 1832 at [33], *per* Simon Brown L.J., cited in *Franbar Holdings Ltd v Casualty Plus Ltd* [2011] EWHC 1161 (Ch) at [39].

CHAPTER 3

APPLICATION OF GENERAL CONTRACTUAL PRINCIPLES

1. AGENCY

Dealers as agents in instalment credit transactions

[*Add at the end of fn.18*]   **3–005**
Brewer v Mann [2012] EWCA Civ 246 at [37].

Agency of necessity

[*Amend fn.30*]   **3–006**
Goff and Jones, *The Law of Unjust Enrichment* (8th edn, 2011), paras 18–50
et seq.

[*Add at the end of fn.31*]
Infolines Public Networks Ltd v Nottingham City Council [2009] EWCA
Civ 708.

[*Add at the end of fn.32*]
ENE 1 Kos Ltd v Petroleo Brasileiro SA Petrobas (The Kos) [2010] 2 Lloyd's
Rep. 409.

4. MISTAKE

Mistake of identity

[*Amend fn.50*]   **3–012**
Treitel, *The Law of Contract* (13th edn, 2011), pp.331–338.

Identity distinguished from attributes

[*Amend fn.58*]   **3–013**
Treitel, *The Law of Contract* (13th edn, 2011), p.335.

Validity of distinction

3–015   [*Amend fn.75*]
Treitel, *The Law of Contract* (13th edn, 2011), pp.332–333.

[*Amend fn.77*]
Treitel, *The Law of Contract* (13th edn, 2011), p.333.

3–021   [*Amend fn.106*]
Treitel, *The Law of Contract* (13th edn, 2011), pp.318–324.

5.   ILLEGALITY

Illegal contracts generally

3–028   [*Amend fn.128*]
Treitel, *The Law of Contract* (13th edn, 2011), pp.471–474.

Effect of illegality on contract

3–029   [*Amend fn.136*]
Treitel, *The Law of Contract* (13th edn, 2011), pp.537–538.

Restitution in illegal contracts

3–031   [*Amend fn.143*]
Treitel, *The Law of Contract* (13th edn, 2011), p.542. Goff and Jones, *The Law of Unjust Enrichment* (8th edn, 2011), Ch.25.

EC competition law

3–041   [*Amend title to*]

EU competition law

[*Amend fn.194*]
Whish, *Competition Law* (7th edn). Wyatt and Dashwood's *European Union Law* (6th edn).

[*fn.209, delete* "Bradley and Child" *and insert*]
Bellamy and Child

[*Add at the end of fn.209*]
Kingdom of Spain v European Commission Case T-398/07.

3–042   **Free movement of goods**

[*Amend fn.210*]
Wyatt and Dashwood's *European Union Law* (6th edn).

Part Two

PROPERTY AND RISK

CHAPTER 4

THE TITLE OF THE SELLER

1.   THE SELLER'S RIGHT TO SELL THE GOODS

4–004

[*Line 7, insert new sentence after* "...criminal law.[21]"]

Because s.12(1) is concerned with defects in the seller's title, the seller will not lack the right to sell the goods merely because a third party has a right to interfere with possession: the interference must be one that "stops or prevents the sale". [21A]

[21A] In *Great Elephant Corp v Trafigura Beheer BV* [2012] EWHC 1745 (Comm), because of irregularities in the loading of a vessel by the seller, a governmental department could refuse cargo documents, the effect of which was to prevent a ship bearing the buyer's oil from leaving port. The department was also able to call upon the navy to take physical steps to prevent departure. The seller was not in breach of the implied term requiring that it have a right to sell (see [92]–[99]).

2.   FREEDOM FROM ENCUMBRANCES AND QUIET POSSESSION

4–026

[*Add at the end of fn.170*]

This sentence was referred to in *Great Elephant Corp v Trafigura Beheer BV* [2012] EWHC 1745 (Comm), where liability did not arise when a governmental minister unlawfully demanded a fine.

4–027

[*fn.182, add at the end of the* Playa Larga *reference*]

Great Elephant Corp v Trafigura Beheer BV [2012] EWHC 1745 (Comm), where the interference occurred after the passing of property, but arose out of circumstances prevailing when the property passed.

CHAPTER 5

PASSING OF PROPERTY

3. GOODS DELIVERED ON APPROVAL OR ON SALE OR RETURN

Approval or on sale or return

5–041   [*Add at the end of fn.214*]
A provision in the contract that goods are subject to inspection by the buyer at any time and place does not make the contract one of sale or return: *Re Redfern Resources Ltd* 2011 BCSC 771 at [52] (Can).

4. UNASCERTAINED GOODS

(a)   *Appropriation with the Assent of the Other Party*

5–073   [*Line 10, insert new fn.391A after the word* "erroneous"]

391A See *Re Redfern Resources Ltd* 2011 BCSC 771 at [46]–[50] (Can).

Conformity with contract

5–085   [*fn.441, insert after the* Pullman *reference*]
Re Redfern Resources Ltd 2011 BCSC 771 at [46]–[50] (Can).

(b)   *Appropriation of Future Goods*

Materials for construction

[*fn.476, after the* Petromec *reference, insert*]
Wincanton Group Ltd v Garbe Logistics UK 1 SARL [2011] EWHC 905 (Ch);

5.   Undivided Shares in Goods Forming Part of a Bulk

Co-ownership of goods

[*Amend fn.614*]
Clerk and Linsell on Torts (20th edn), paras 17.68–17.70

6.   Reservation of the Right of Disposal

[*Add at the end of fn.653*]
Consequently, a reservation of title clause expressed to apply until "full payment" was received continued fully to bind the goods even though the buyer had paid part of the price: *Wincanton Group Ltd v Garbe Logistics UK 1 SARL* [2011] EWHC 905 (Ch), where the court did not have to deal with the question whether a seller in administration might be compelled to accept payment of any sum owed by the part-paying buyer.

[*Add at the end of fn.832*]
See *Hachette UK Ltd v Borders (UK) Ltd* [2009] EWHC 3487 (Ch).

[*Add at the end of the text*]
Notwithstanding a buyer's entry into insolvent administration, an administrator will not be required to apply to the court under para.72 to dispose of goods if the goods were supplied under a continuing authority conferred upon the buyer to dispose of the goods in the course of its business.[837A]

[837A] *Sandhu v Jetstar Retail Ltd* [2011] EWCA Civ 459. In this case, the buyer's authority to resell had not been revoked. Moreover, the goods had been supplied on easy credit terms (only five per cent of the price had to be paid 60 days after delivery), which pointed to the goods being permissibly resold notwithstanding the buyer's insolvency. Since the case concerned, as a preliminary issue, the buyer's authority to resell, the court did not resolve the seller's claim that it might recover the price of the goods as an expense of the administration. The language of Insolvency Act 1986, Sch.B1 para.99(3) and Insolvency Rules (SI 1986/1925) r.2.67 suggests that the seller's claim might not have been a straightforward one, since the contract was concluded and the goods supplied prior to the buyer entering into administration. This conclusion in turn suggests that a court should only in exceptional cases conclude that the buyer's authority to resell is a continuing one.

Disadvantages of a *Romalpa* clause

5–170   [*Amend fn.868*]
See also (on VAT) Value Added Tax Regulations 1995 (SI 1995/2518), reg.55V (added by the Value Added Tax (Amendment) (No.2) Regulations 2002 (SI 2002/1142))

CHAPTER 6

RISK AND FRUSTRATION

1. RISK

(c)   *Carriage of Goods to the Buyer*

Seller's responsibilities at point of delivery

[*Add at the end of the text*]   **6–019**

In *KG Bominflot Bunkergesellschaft fur Mineraloele mbH & Co AG v Petroplus Marketing AG (The Mercini Lady)*,[106A] the buyer's argument was not that the goods (a cargo of gasoil) should be shipped in a condition that they would endure a normal voyage, but rather that they should for the duration of the voyage and for a reasonable time thereafter be of satisfactory quality and adhere to their contractual specification. This was an attempt to set up a "continuing" rather than a "prospective" warranty.[106B] The buyer's argument, particularly on satisfactory quality, was inconsistent with s.14(1) of the Sale of Goods Act, which provides that there is no implied term in a sale of goods contract concerning quality and fitness except as set out in ss.14–15 of the Act, and the court ultimately dismissed the buyer's argument on that ground.[106C] But the buyer's argument failed for additional reasons. It was inconsistent with a contractual provision that an inspection conducted at the loading port was binding on the parties,[106D] and moreover its "elusive" character made it difficult for the buyer to frame in a satisfactory way.[106E] The buyer's admission that the goods were within specification on shipment appeared also to be inconsistent with the risk being on the buyer from shipment.[106F]

[106A] [2010] EWCA Civ 1145; [2011] 1 Lloyd's Rep 442.
[106B] *ibid.*, at [18].

[106C] *ibid.*, at [45].
[106D] *ibid.*, at [40].
[106E] *ibid.*, at [23].
[106F] *ibid.*, at [16].

CHAPTER 7

TRANSFER OF TITLE BY NON-OWNERS

1.   IN GENERAL

Remedies of the owner

[*Amend fn.10*]   **7–002**
Clerk and Linsell on Torts (20th edn), paras 30.14–30.15

[*Amend fn.12*]
Clerk and Linsell on Torts (20th edn), para.17.107.

5.   MERCANTILE AGENTS

[*Add at the end of fn.316*]   **7–047**
Angara Maritime Ltd v Oceanconnect UK Ltd [2010] EWHC 619 (QB).

6.   SELLER IN POSSESSION

Possession of seller

[*Add in fn.363 after the* Forsythe *reference*]   **7–057**
Angara Maritime Ltd v Oceanconnect UK Ltd [2010] EWHC 619 (QB)

Delivery or transfer

[*Add at the end of fn.384*]   **7–062**

See also *Angara Maritime Ltd v Oceanconnect UK Ltd* [2010] EWHC 619 (QB) (while a charterer redelivering a vessel would voluntarily deliver bunkers to the shipowner, the charterer would not if the shipowner withdrew the vessel from hire).

10.   LIMITATION

Property obtained through unlawful conduct

7–117   [*Line 2, delete the phrase in round brackets* "(in England and Wales, the Director of the Asset Recovery Agency)"]

Part Three

PERFORMANCE OF THE CONTRACT

CHAPTER 8

DELIVERY

1.   IN GENERAL

Delivery and payment

[Add after the first sentence]   **8–004**
Where the contract is silent about the order of contractual performance in general, "performance of one obligation will only be a condition precedent to another obligation where either the first obligation must for practical reasons clearly be performed before the second obligation can arise or the second obligation is the direct quid pro quo of the first, in the sense that only performance of the first earns entitlement to the second".[18A]

[18A] *Astrazeneca UK Ltd v Albemarle International Corp* [2011] EWHC 1574 (Comm) at [250]; [2011] 2 CLC 252.

[Add at the end of the text]
The seller may retain possession of the goods indefinitely pending payment of the price.[27A]

[27A] *Lomas v JFB Firth Rixson Inc* [2012] EWCA Civ 419 at [34]–[35].

2. METHODS OF DELIVERY

How delivery effected

8–007   [*Add at the end of fn.45*]
Where a seller under a work and materials contract is to install goods on the buyer's premises, delivery might not occur prior to the installation of the goods: *Wincanton Group Ltd v Garbe Logistics UK 1 SARL* [2011] EWHC 905 (Ch).

3. PLACE OF DELIVERY

Delivery at buyer's premises

8–023   [*Delete the last sentence of the text and insert*]
Furthermore, the person receiving the goods may be unknown to the buyer and have no actual or apparent authority from the buyer to receive the goods, yet be someone whom the person effecting delivery would expect to have authority to receive the goods.[117] The risk of some "apparently respectable person" gaining access to the buyer's premises, signing for the goods and making off with them therefore falls on the buyer.[117A]

[117A] *Galbraith and Grant Ltd v Block* [1922] 2 KB 155 at p.157.
   [*fn.117 remains the same*]

4. TIME OF DELIVERY

Notice making time of the essence

8–026   [*At the end of the first sentence insert new fn.129A*]

[129A] In the light of intermediate stipulation analysis, there is a need to "adapt" equity's belief that the common law always treated the time of performance as being of the essence of the contract: *Samarenko v Dawn Hill House Ltd* [2011] EWCA Civ 1445 at [39]; [2012] 1 P & CR 14.

[*Add to fn.137 after the* Dalkia *reference*]
   Multi Veste 226 BV v NI Summer Row Unitholder BV [2011] EWHC 2026 (Ch); *Samarenko v Dawn Hill House Ltd* [2011] EWCA Civ 1445 at [37]; [2012] 1 P & CR 14. In *Samarenko*, Lewison L.J. at [42] criticises his own earlier judgment in *Multi Veste* on the ground that it may have been too "prescriptive". In *Multi Veste*, when considering the effect of serving a notice, the court does appear to suggest at [201] that the notice itself might change the underlying common law position: "I conclude therefore that the service of notice making time of the essence changes the question from whether delay amounts to a repudiation to the question whether

failure to perform the obligation at all amounts to a repudiation." It is submitted that these words should be treated with some caution (see *Samarenko v Dawn Hill House Ltd* [2011] EWCA Civ 1445 at [65]; [2012] 1 P & CR 14).

6.   DELIVERY BY INSTALMENTS

Repudiation by renunciation

[*Add to fn.370 after the* Seadrill *reference*]   **8–078**
Eminence Property Developments Ltd v Heaney [2010] EWCA Civ 1168; [2011] 2 All E.R. (Comm) 223.

[*Add at the end of fn.379*]
Eminence Property Developments Ltd v Heaney [2010] EWCA Civ 1168; [2011] 2 All E.R. (Comm) 223.

[*Add to fn.390 after the* Maple Flock *reference*]   **8–081**
In *Astrazeneca UK Ltd v Albemarle International Corp* [2011] EWHC 1574 (Comm) at [261]: [2011] 2 CLC 252, which concerned a requirements contract with a minimum duration of three years, it was said that the seller's failure to deliver one, possibly even two, instalments would not amount to a repudiatory breach. Emphasis was laid upon the long-term character of the contract.

7.   CLAUSES EXCUSING DELIVERY

[*Add to fn.432 after the* Navrom *reference*]   **8–089**
Dunavant Enterprises Inc v Olympia Spinning & Weaving Mills Ltd [2011] EWHC 1128 (Comm); [2011] 2 Lloyd's Rep. 619; *Gardiner v Agricultural and Rural Finance Pty Ltd* [2007] NSWCA 235 at [56].

"Prevented" clauses

[*Insert at the end of fn.448*]   **8–092**
Dunavant Enterprises Inc v Olympia Spinning & Weaving Mills Ltd [2011] EWHC 1128 (Comm); [2011] 2 Lloyd's Rep. 619.

"Hindered"

[*Add to fn.459 after the* Phosphate *reference*]   **8–094**
Holcim (Singapore) Pte Ltd v Precise Development Pte Ltd [2011] SGCA 1 at [51] (Sing).

[*Add to the end of fn.463*]
cf. *Holcim (Singapore) Pte Ltd v Precise Development Pte Ltd* [2011] SGCA 1 at [52]–[53] (leaving open "astronomical" increase) (Sing).

[*Insert new fn.463A at the end of the text*]

463A *Holcim (Singapore) Pte Ltd v Precise Development Pte Ltd* [2011] SGCA 1 at [54]–[60] (Sing).

8–099   [*Insert in fn.498 after the* Brauer *reference*]
Thames Valley Power Ltd v Total Gas & Power Ltd [2005] EWHC 2208 (Comm) at [50]; [2006] 1 Lloyd's Rep 441.

CHAPTER 9

ACCEPTANCE AND PAYMENT

1. ACCEPTANCE

Meaning of "acceptance"

[*fn.4, replace* "34A" *with* "35A"]   **9–002**

Acceptance and taking delivery

[*Add after the first sentence of fn.9*]   **9–003**
Re Redfern Resources Ltd 2011 BCSC 771 at [53] (Can) ("'Acceptance' means both the physical receipt of the goods by a buyer and the legal duty of the buyer to accept goods properly delivered by the seller").

2. PAYMENT

Default in payment

[*Insert after the sentence ending with fn.146*]   **9–027**
If time is not of the essence, but the seller's duty to deliver is conditional upon the buyer paying the price, the seller has the further option of suspending delivery indefinitely until payment is made.[146A]

[146A] *Lomas v JFR Firth Rixson Inc* [2012] EWCA Civ 419 at [34]–[35].

(a) *Methods of Payment*

Internet payments

[*Delete the following text in lines 20–22* "the Consumer Protection (Distance   **9–036**
Selling Regulations) 2000,[192] the Financial Services (Distance Marketing) Regulations 2004[193]", *together with fnn.192–193, and insert*]

the Payment Services Regulations 2009[192–193]

[192–193] SI 2009/209, reg.61. See below, paras 14–058 and 14–061.

(c) *Time of Payment*

Time of payment specified

9–051   [*Add at the end of fn.248*]
See also *Dominion Corporate Trustees Ltd v Debenhams Properties Ltd* [2010] EWHC 1193 (Ch).

Time for payment of deposit

9–052   [*Insert in fn.256 after the* Portaria *reference*]
Samarenko v Dawn Hill House Ltd [2011] EWCA Civ 1445 at [37]; [2012] 1 P & CR 14.

[*Insert in fn.259 after the* Damon *reference*]
Samarenko v Dawn Hill House Ltd [2011] EWCA Civ 1445; [2012] 1 P & CR 14.

Part Four

DEFECTIVE GOODS

CHAPTER 10

CLASSIFICATION OF STATEMENTS AS TO GOODS

3.   MISREPRESENTATIONS INDUCING THE CONTRACT

Misrepresentations inducing the contract

[*Amend fn.40*]   **10–008**
Treitel, *The Law of Contract* (13th edn, 2011), para.6–013.

Right to rescind in equity

[*Add at the end of fn.53*]   **10–009**
See also in general Treitel, *The Law of Contract* (13th edn, 2011), para.9–013.

[*Amend fn.56*]
Treitel, *The Law of Contract* (13th edn, 2011), para.9–023.

[*Amend fn.58*]
Treitel, *The Law of Contract* (13th edn, 2011), paras 9–023 *et seq*.

[*fn.58, delete the reference to* Goff and Jones, *The Law of Restitution*]

[*Amend fn.63*]
Treitel, *The Law of Contract* (13th edn, 2011) para.9–136.

[*Amend fn.64*]
Treitel, *The Law of Contract* (13th edn, 2011) para.9–148.

6. CONDITIONS

Conditions: difficulty of term

10–024   [*Amend fn.146*]
Treitel, *The Law of Contract* (13th edn, 2011), paras 2–103 *et seq.*

Promises with regard to conditions

10–025   [*Add at the end of fn.149*]
For a recent discussion of this topic see *UR Power GmbH v Kuok Oils and Grains Pte Ltd* [2009] EWHC 1940 (Comm); [2009] 2 Lloyd's Rep.495 at [11] *et seq.*

7. INTERMEDIATE TERMS

Intermediate term?

10–033   [*Add at the end of fn.187*]
See also *GB Gas Holdings Ltd v Accenture (UK) Ltd* [2010] EWCA Civ 912.

[*Add at the end of fn.190*]
; and see *GB Gas Holdings Ltd v Accenture (UK) Ltd* [2010] EWCA Civ 912 where the question is discussed in connection with the specific terms of a written contract.

Differences of approach: commercial disputes

10–035   [*fn.197, delete the reference to* Treitel, *The Law of Contract*]

Examples of conditions

10–037   [*Add at the end of fn.214*]
See also *RG Grain Trade LLP v Feed Factors International Ltd* [2011] EWHC 1889 (Comm); [2011] 2 Lloyd's Rep. 432, where arbitrators were found to have assumed (wrongly) that any quality term must be a condition.

CHAPTER 11

TERMS AS TO DESCRIPTION AND QUALITY IMPLIED
BY THE SALE OF GOODS ACT

1. CORRESPONDENCE WITH DESCRIPTION

Sale not by description

[Add at the end of fn.52] **11–011**
There is discussion in a recent hire purchase case concerning the description of a vintage car, *Brewer v Mann* [2012] EWCA Civ 246; but the true analysis of the words used was not settled, the matter being remitted for retrial.

Words of description and warranties

[Add at the end of fn.66] **11–013**
See also *RG Grain Trade LLP v Feed Factors International Ltd* [2011] EWHC 1889 (Comm); [2011] 2 Lloyd's Rep.432, where a statement argued to relate to quality was remitted to arbitrators to determine whether it was a condition, a warranty or an intermediate term.

Form of contract

[Add at the end of fn.75] **11–015**
See also *RG Grain Trade LLP v Feed Factors International Ltd* [2011] EWHC 1889 (Comm); [2011] 2 Lloyd's Rep. 432, where part of a specification was remitted to arbitrators to determine whether it was a condition, a warranty or an intermediate term.

Failure of goods to "correspond with description": first type of case

[Add at the end of fn.92] **11–018**
See below, para.11–089 as to a (rejected) argument that there could be an implied term that the goods would remain within their specification over a period.

Second type of case

11–019   [*Add at the end of fn.107*]
; *cf. Brewer v Mann* [2012] EWCA CIV (hire purchase: car sold as "1930 Speed Six Bentley" actually contained 1927 reconstructed standard 6.5 litre engine: still complied with description (see at [307]).

2.   QUALITY AND FITNESS FOR PURPOSE

(b)   *Satisfactory Quality*

"Sells goods in the course of a business"

11–027   [*Add at the end of fn.149*]
; *MacDonald v Pollock (The Monaco)* [2012] CSIH 12; [2012] 1 Lloyd's Rep.425 (ship).

Durability

11–040   [*Line 9, delete* "Even assuming that this exists as a special implied term for most sales, the fact that" *and insert*]
Doubt has however been cast recently on the possibility of any such implied term,[205A] and despite the fact that the term "durability" has a consumer orientation, it is submitted that

[205A] *KB Bominflot Bunkergesellschaft für Mineralöle mbH v Petroplus Marketing AG (The Mercini Lady)* [2010] EWCA Civ 1145; [2011] 1 Lloyd's Rep. 442, where however the term argued for related to ability to retain contractual specification till arrival and a reasonable time thereafter. It was in fact said to be one of prospective rather than continuing effect, though some of what is reported as having been said in argument causes doubt about this. See also above, paras 11–089, 11–067; below, paras 18–297, 18–298.

[*Delete the last sentence of fn.205*]

First exception: defects specifically drawn to buyer's attention

11–041   [*Insert new fn.211A at end of line 8, after* "satisfactory quality"]

[211A] See however *Stephenson v Cookson* [2009] EWCA Civ 1270 (horse: different defect from that to which attention had been drawn).

Second exception: examination of goods

11–042   [*Add at the beginning of fn.218*]
MacDonald v Pollock (The Monaco) [2012] CSIH 12; [2012] 1 Lloyd's Rep.425 (ship: relevant examination was that actually conducted).

Examples

[Add at the end of the first sentence of fn.226]   **11–044**
; *Balmoral Group Ltd v Borealis (UK) Ltd* [2006] EWHC 1900 (Comm); [2006]
2 Lloyd's Rep. 629 (polymer).

[Add at the end of fn.226]
(Supply and of Goods and Services Act 1982: goods liable to be downgraded
under EU animal by-products regulations).

[Add at the end of fn.228]
Contrast *Lowe v W Machell Joinery Ltd* [2011] EWCA Civ 794; [2012] 1 All
E.R. (Comm) 153 (staircase supplied as specified but did not comply with
Building Regulations, though change to specification required would have been
very slight: not satisfactory).

[Amend fn.233]
Egan v Motor Services (Bath) Ltd [2008] 1 All E.R. 1156n

[In the penultimate line of the text change "win (with caution)" *to* "will (with
caution)"]

(c)   *Fitness for Purpose*

**"Expressly or by implication makes known . . . to the seller . . . any
particular purpose for which the goods are being bought"**

[Add at the end of fn.286]   **11–055**
; *BSS Group Plc v Makers (UK) Ltd* [2011] EWCA Civ 809; [2011] T.C.L.R. 7
(requirement for "Uponor" parts).

"Reasonably fit for that purpose"

[Add at the end of fn.312]   **11–057**
; *Crozier v A & P Canada Inc* (2010) 329 D.L.R. (4th) 565 (peanut butter:
claimant had long history of Crohn's disease).

Related contracts

[In the last sentence of the text, delete "But it can be argued" *and insert]*   **11–069**
It has been argued

[Add new sentence at the end of the text]
But cases continue to be decided on the basis of the strict liability of the Sale of
Goods Act or by analogy with it.[367A]

[367A] *e.g. Kingsway Hall Hotel Ltd Red Sky IT (Hounslow) Ltd* [2010] EWHC 965
(TCC); (2010) 26 Const. L.J. 542 (reservation system for hotel not satisfactory).

Cf. Southwark LBC v IBM UK Ltd [2011] EWHC 549 (TCC); 135 Con. L.R. 136 (no sale involved in provision of third party software and associated services).

3. SALE BY SAMPLE

Written contract

11–076   [*Amend fn.390*]
Treitel, *The Law of Contract* (13th edn, 2011), para.6–013.

4. OTHER IMPLIED TERMS

Other implied terms

11–089   [*Insert after the first sentence*]
. . . [relevant] and by virtue of the preliminary statement as to implied warranties in s.14(1) excludes others. Thus an implied term that goods shipped are capable of remaining within their contractual specification till arrival and a reasonable time thereafter has been rejected, and the judgment casts doubt on the possibility of other implied terms to similar effect.[436A]

[436A] *KB Bominflot Bunkergesellschaft für Mineralöle mbH v Petroplus Marketing AG (The Mercini Lady)* [2010] EWCA Civ 1145; [2011] 1 Lloyd's Rep. 442. A major ground for refusal to make such an implication was the presence of detailed provisions for analysis on loading. The term argued for was said to be one of prospective rather than continuing effect, though some of what is said in argument causes doubt about this. See also above, para.11–089; below, paras 18–297, 18–298.

[*Amend fn.440*]
Treitel, *The Law of Contract* (13th edn, 2011), paras 6–031 *et seq.*

[*Add at the end of fn.440*]
Attorney General of Belize v Belize Telecom Ltd [2009] UKPC 10; [2009] 1 W.L.R. 1988.

CHAPTER 12

REMEDIES IN RESPECT OF DEFECTS

1. MISREPRESENTATION

Powers of court under Misrepresentation Act 1967 section 2(2)

[*Amend fn.14*]   **12–004**
Treitel, *The Law of Contract* (13th edn, 2011), para.9–071.

Restitutio in integrum impossible

[*Amend fn.27*]   **12–007**
Treitel, *The Law of Contract* (13th edn, 2011), para.9–097.

Liability in tort: deceit

[*Add at the end of fn.59*]
Treitel, *The Law of Contract* (13th edn, 2011), para.9–062.   **12–012**

Negligent misrepresentation

[*Amend fn.71*]   **12–013**
Clerk and Lindsell on Torts (20th edn, 2010), paras 8–91 *et seq.*

[*Add at the end of fn.71*]
Treitel, *The Law of Contract* (13th edn, 2011) paras 9–033 *et seq.*

Damages recoverable

[*Amend fn.82*]   **12–015**
Treitel, *The Law of Contract* (13th edn, 2011), para.9–066.

"Fiction of fraud"

12–016 [*Amend fn.83*]
Clerk and Lindsell on Torts (20th edn, 2010), paras 18–27, 18–28.

[*Amend fn.87*]
Treitel, *The Law of Contract* (13th edn, 2011), para.9–043 fn.207.

2.   BREACH OF CONTRACTUAL TERM

Anticipatory breach

12–021 [*In fn.104, add Report reference for* SK Shipping]
[2010] 2 Lloyd's Rep. 158.

Failure of performance: breach of condition

12–022 [*Add at the end of fn.120*]
In *RG Grain Trade LLP v Factors International Ltd* [2011] EWHC 1889 (Comm); [2011] 2 Lloyd's Rep. 432 it was said that it was not the law that there was a right of rejection for quality matters unless the contract provides otherwise: at [42].

What constitutes rejection

12–034 [*Add at end of fn.181*]
MacDonald v Pollock (The Monaco) [2012] CSIH 12; [2012] 1 Lloyd's Rep. 425 (ship).

Restitution: recovery of money paid

12–069 [*Amend fn.410*]
Goff and Jones, *The Law of Unjust Enrichment* (8th edn, 2011), paras 12–16 *et seq*.

Failure of consideration must be total

12–070 [*Amend fn.420*]
Goff and Jones, *The Law of Unjust Erichment* (8th edn, 2011), para.3–18.

[*Amend fn.422*]
Goff and Jones, *The Law of Unjust Erichment* (8th edn, 2011), paras 13–31 *et seq*.

[*Amend fn.423*]
Goff and Jones, *The Law of Unjust Erichment* (8th edn, 2011), paras 12–16 *et seq*.

3. Additional Rights of Buyer in Consumer Cases

Power to require repair or replacement

[6th line from bottom of paragraph, change "will not be open" *to* "may not   **12–079**
always be open"*]*

[5th line from bottom of paragraph, change "these are conditioned" *to* "these
are sometimes conditioned"*]*

Exercise of the power

[Replace the last sentence of the third paragraph of 12–081 beginning "Second,   **12–081**
it is provided . . ." *with]*
    As to disproportion, the only guidance is given (in s.48B(4)) in connection with
the comparative merits of repair and replacement, and nothing further is said relevant to s.48B(3)(c).[451A]

[451A] See further below, para.12–108.

"Disproportionate"

[In line 3, replace "whichever other Part 5A remedy" *with* "whichever other of   **12–082**
the two remedies, repair and replacement,"*]*

Replacement—meaning

[Insert new fn.455A at the end of the first sentence]   **12–084**

[455A] The CJEU has, in a case on the Directive itself, *Gebr Weber GmbH v Wittmer*
Joined Cases C-65/09 and C-87/09 [2011] 3 C.M.L.R.27, confirmed that the cost
of replacement lies on the buyer, and comes under the words "necessary costs"
even where it was the seller who had (correctly) installed the goods (tiles). This
was confirmed by the fact that the Directive requires replacement "free of charge"
(though this does not appear in the Regulations). However, it appears to suggest
that considerations of proportionality could lead to the reduction of the sum
payable, which might in turn lead to availability of the remedies of reduction of
price and rescission. It is not easy to see any warrant for such a route to what may
be called the second tier remedies in the Regulations, or perhaps the Directive.

Damages for loss of use during repair or replacement

[Add at the end of fn.464]   **12–088**
    The decision is in fact based on the requirement of repair or replacement "free
of charge" in the Directive, words which do not appear in the UK Regulations.

Rejection at common law

[Add at the end of fn.483]   **12–098**

In *Lowe v W Machell Joinery Ltd* [2011] EWCA Civ 794; [2012] 1 All
E.R. (Comm) 153 it was assumed that the common law remedy of rejection
remains open to a person who does not pursue the statutory remedies: see at
[51]–[52].

[*Add at the end of fn.484*]
See also below, fn.486.

Statutory rescission: requirements

12–099   [*Alter reference in line 1 of fn.486 from* "s.27E(3)(a)" *to*]
s.48E(3)(a)

[*Change cross-reference in fn.490 to*]
. . . above, para.12–088.

Priority among the Part 5A remedies

12–108   [*Delete all main text in the paragraph after the indented quotation on p.652,
and substitute the following*]
Although the words "in the first place"[507] are not found in Part 5A, it would
seem obvious that in practice cure or replacement must be considered by the
buyer before the more drastic remedies or reduction of the price and (especially)
rescission. Where both repair and replacement are impossible, the position as to
what happens next is stated in s.48B(3)(a): the seller "must" not require repair or
replacement, and hence what may be called the second tier remedies are available.
But in the Directive the requirement to ask whether the remedy is *disproportionate* (as opposed to impossible) operates only "in comparison with the alternative remedy", *i.e.* repair or replacement.[508] So whether anything else entitles the
seller to move to the second tier remedies is not clear. The UK Regulations,
however, add specifically (in s.48B(3)(c)) that the seller "must" not require the
seller to repair, or as the case may be, replace the goods, not only where the
remedy is impossible, but also if it "is . . . disproportionate in comparison to"
reduction of the price or rescission. This means that under the Regulations the
seller need not always require repair or replacement, and indeed, to use the words
of s.48B(3), actually *must* not do so in the circumstances of disproportionality
indicated. These are not however further described, since as stated above the indication of when a remedy is disproportionate is only given as between the remedies
of repair and replacement. This matter is then returned to in s.48C(1)and (2),
whereby the seller may reduce the price or rescind, not only if repair or replacement is impossible, or has been demanded but has not occurred, but also where
"by virtue of section 48B(3) above the buyer may require neither" reduction of the
price nor rescission. It would seem clear that if the buyer *must* not require repair
or replacement in certain situations of disproportionality, it is also correct to say
that he *may* not do so, and hence that there may sometimes be a route to the
second tier remedies without a demand of repair or replacement or impossibility

of such remedies. Whether this route to the second tier remedies was intended by those responsible for the Directive or not, it seems to be what the UK Regulations prescribe.[509]

[508] This is emphasised in *Gebr Weber GmbH v Wittmer* Joined Cases C-65/09 and C-87/09 [2011] 3 C.M.L.R.27: see above, para.12–084.
 [fnn.507 and 509 remain the same]

4. Misrepresentations Subsequently Incorporated into the Contract

Practical difficulties

[Amend fn.540]   **12–122**
Treitel, *The Law of Contract* (13th edn, 2011), para.9–093.

5. Tort Liability in Respect of Goods

Tort action against seller

[Amend fn.547]   **12–123**
Clerk and Lindsell on Torts (20th edn, 2010), paras 2–141 *et seq.*

[Amend fn.548]
Clerk and Lindsell on Torts (20th edn, 2010), paras 32–07 *et seq.*

[Amend fn.550]
Treitel, *The Law of Contract* (13th edn, 2011), paras 20–124 *et seq.*

Economic loss: goods which threaten damage or are otherwise unsatisfactory

[Amend fn.565]   **12–128**
Clerk and Lindsell on Torts (20th edn, 2010), paras 8–125 *et seq.*

[Amend fn.568]
Clerk and Lindsell on Torts (20th edn, 2010), paras 8–128 *et seq.*

[Amend fn.569]
Clerk and Lindsell on Torts (20th edn, 2010), paras 8–95 *et seq.*

6.   MISTAKE AS TO SUBJECT MATTER OF CONTRACT

Mistake

12–130   [*Amend fn.573*]
Treitel, *The Law of Contract* (13th edn, 2011), paras 8–002 *et seq*.

CHAPTER 13

EXEMPTION CLAUSES

2.   BASIC PRINCIPLES OF FORMATION OF
CONTRACT APPLIED TO EXEMPTION CLAUSES

All basic principles of formation applicable in sale

[*Amend fn.30*]   **13–012**
Macdonald, *Exemption Clauses and Unfair Terms* (2nd edn, 2006)
Lewison, *The Interpretation of Contracts* (5th edn, 2011)

[*Add at the end of fn.30*]
; McMeel, *The Construction of Contracts: Interpretation, Implication and
Rectification* (2nd edn, 2011).

Clause incorporated in contract but nevertheless inoperative at
common law

[*Add at the end of fn.46*]   **13–016**
For a recent discussion of the *Curtis* case see Rix L.J. in *Axa Sun Life Services
Plc v Campbell Martin Ltd* [2011] EWCA Civ 133; [2011] 2 Lloyd's Rep. 1 at
[99]–[105].

[*Add at the end of fn.52*]
The case was however disapproved on this point in *Astrazeneca UK Ltd v
Albemarle International Corp* [2011] EWHC 1574 (Comm); [2011] 2 C.L.C. 252
at [274] *et seq.* (sale of chemicals).

Third parties

[*Amend fn.55*]   **13–017**
Treitel, *The Law of Contract* (13th edn, 2011), paras 14–057 *et seq.*

Contracts (Rights of Third Parties) Act 1999

13–018   *[Amend fn.65]*
Treitel, *The Law of Contract* (13th edn, 2011), paras 14–090 *et seq.*

3.   INTERPRETATION OF EXEMPTION CLAUSES

Strict interpretation

13–020   *[Amend fn.73]*
Treitel, *The Law of Contract* (13th edn, 2011), paras 7–014 *et seq.*

Negligence

13–022   *[Add at the end of fn.93]*
As to the meaning of gross negligence, see *Camerata Property Inc v Credit Suisse Securities (Europe) Ltd* [2011] EWHC 479 (Comm); [2011] 2 B.C.L.C.54.

[Amend fn.96]
Treitel, *The Law of Contract* (13th edn, 2011), paras 7–034 *et seq.*

Exclusion of warranties

13–025   *[Delete last two lines of fn.111 (reference to* KB Bominflot *case)]*

[Add at the end of fn.116]
In *KB Bominflot Bunkergesellschaft für Mineralöle mbH & Co v Petroplus Marketing AG* [2010] EWCA Civ 1145; [2011] 1 Lloyd's Rep. 2011 it was held in connection with a bulk sale of oil that effective exclusion of conditions requires the use of that specific word. But in *Air Transworld Ltd v Bombardier Inc* [2012] EWHC 243 (Comm); [2012] 1 Lloyd's Rep. 349 a very widely drawn clause in a sale of an aircraft excluding normal terms and substituting its own regime was held effective despite the actual word not appearing (as opposed to the word "warranty").

A different approach

13–031   *[Add at the end of fn.156]*
The *Morgan Chase* case, concerning an investment contract, was affirmed on appeal sub nom. *Springwell Navigation Corp v JP Morgan Chase Bank* [2010] EWCA 1221; [2010] 2 C.L.C. 705, which contains further important general discussion of the problem of entire agreement clauses.

[Insert immediately before fn.157]
[. . . which are considered below] under the heading of Control of Exemption Clauses by Statute. [The recent . . .]

[Insert new sentence in main text after fn.159]

As regards interpretation, the different wordings of such clauses make it difficult to generalise. But in general such a clause may exclude collateral warranties,[159A] but not implied terms[159B] or, unless their wording is clear, liability for precontractual representations whether fraudulent or not.[159C] But in any case [there must be a limit to this: . . .] *[run on to main text after these words]*

[159A] See, *e.g. The Procter & Gamble Co v Svenska Cellulosa Aktiebolaget SCA* [2012] EWHC 498 (Ch) (holding also that claim for rectification not excluded). See further below, para.13–057.
[159B] *e.g. Compass Group UK and Ireland Ltd v Mid-Essex Hospital Services NHS Trust* [2012] EWHC 781 (QB).
[159C] See *Axa Sun Life Services Plc v Campbell Martin Ltd* [2011] EWCA Civ 133; [2011] 2 Lloyd's Rep.1 at [91]–[95] (insurance representative agreement: full discussion of such clauses).

[Add at the end of fn.161]

As to this case see Rix L.J. in *Axa Sun Life Services Plc v Campbell Martin Ltd* [2011] EWCA Civ 133; [2011] 2 Lloyd's Rep. 1 at [99]–[105].

Exclusion of conditions, warranties and liabilities express or implied

[Add at the end of fn.166]   **13–032**

In *Air Transworld Ltd v Bombardier Inc* [2012] EWHC 243 (Comm); [2012] 1 Lloyd's Rep. 349 a very widely drawn clause in the sale of an aircraft excluding normal terms and substituting its own regime was held effective, on the basis that "No one reading the provision could be in any doubt that that it was intended that the obligations resting on the seller . . . were to be found only in [certain documents]" (at [27] *et seq.*). Such schemes appear quite common in large scale commercial contracts, including construction contracts, and the existence of the alternative scheme may, if it is itself reasonable, make exclusions of the normal terms reasonable.

Clauses limiting the damages recoverable

[Amend fn.199]   **13–037**

Treitel, *The Law of Contract* (13th edn, 2011), paras 20–130 *et seq.*

Exclusion of indirect or consequential loss

[Amend fn.215]   **13–038**

Treitel, *The Law of Contract* (13th edn, 2011), para.7–017.

Arbitration clauses

[Amend fn.245, delete "Mustill and Boyd, *Commercial Arbitration*" *and insert]*   **13–042**

Redfern and Hunter, *Law and Practice of International Commercial Arbitration* (4th edn)

4. DOCTRINE OF FUNDAMENTAL BREACH

Doctrine of fundamental breach

13–043   [*Amend fn.254*]
Treitel, *The Law of Contract* (13th edn, 2011), paras 7–024 *et seq*.

Doctrine as a rule of law

13–045   [*Amend fn.259*]
Treitel, *The Law of Contract* (13th edn, 2011), para.7–021.

Rule of law held to survive in different form

13–047   [*Amend fn.266*]
Goff and Jones, *The Law of Unjust Enrichment* (8th edn, 2011), para.3–33.

***George Mitchell v Finney Lock Seeds Ltd*: doctrine no longer exists as separate entity**

13–049   [*Amend fn.286*]
Tercon Contractors Ltd v British Columbia [2010] 1 S.C.R. 69.

Deliberate breach

13–053   [*Add at the end of fn.303*]
A presumption that an exemption clause should not cover a deliberate breach is however specifically rejected in *Astrazeneca UK Ltd v Albemarle International Corp* [2011] EWHC 1574 (Comm); [2011] 2 C.L.C. 252 at [274] *et seq*. (sale of chemicals).

5. CONTROL OF EXEMPTION CLAUSES BY STATUTE

Entire agreement clauses

13–057   [*Add at the end of fn.316*]
See also above, para.13–031.

Non-reliance provisions

13–058   [*Add at the end of fn.320*]
The *Morgan Chase* case was affirmed on appeal sub nom. *Springwell Navigation Corp v JP Morgan Chase Bank* [2010] EWCA 1221; [2010] 2 C.L.C.705; the *Titan Steel Wheels* case is now reported at [2011] 2 Lloyd's Rep. 92.

[*Add in the penultimate line of fn.321, immediately after "465"*]
; *Axa Sun Life Services Plc v Campbell Martin Ltd* [2011] EWCA Civ 133; [2011] 2 Lloyd's Rep. 1 at [48]–[51] [caught by. . .].

[*Add at the end of fn.322*]
The problem is extensively discussed by Christopher Clarke J. in *Raiffeisen Zentralbank Österreich AG v Royal Bank of Scotland Plc* [2010] EWHC 1392; [2011] 1 Lloyd's Rep. 123 at [274] *et seq.*, the upshot of the discussion being not dissimilar to the view advanced here. See also *Axa Sun Life Services Plc v Campbell Martin Ltd* [2011] EWCA Civ 133; [2011] 2 Lloyd's Rep. 1 at [51]; and a useful discussion in *Clerk and Lindsell on Torts* (20th edn, 2010), para.8–125.

Reasonableness

[*Add at the end of fn.332*]   **13–061**
Axa Sun Life Services Plc v Campbell Martin Ltd [2011] EWCA Civ 133; [2011] 2 Lloyd's Rep. 1.

Types of clause covered

[*Amend fn.367*]   **13–067**
Titan Steel Wheels Ltd v Royal Bank of Scotland Plc [2011] 2 Lloyd's Rep. 92.

Use in the Unfair Contract Terms Act

[*Add at the end of fn.389*]   **13–075**
Contrast *Air Transworld Ltd v Bombardier Inc* [2012] EWHC 243 (Comm); [2012] 1 Lloyd's Rep. 349 (company used as vehicle, but in respect of the particular contract having the function of owning and operating aircraft, held to be buying in the course of a business).

Goods "of a type ordinarily supplied for private use or consumption"

[*Add at the end of fn.405*]   **13–082**
; *Air Transworld Ltd v Bombardier Inc* [2012] EWHC 243 (Comm); [2012] 1 Lloyd's Rep. 349 (Challenger 605 aircraft often bought for private use).

Present wording

[*Add at the end of fn.456*]   **13–091**
; *Air Transworld Ltd v Bombardier Inc* [2012] EWHC 243 (Comm); [2012] 1 Lloyd's Rep. 349, where an elaborate scheme of duties effectively superseding the normal duties of a seller in a contract for the sale of an aircraft was held reasonable on the general basis that commercial parties should be free to negotiate their own terms.

[*Add at the end of fn.458*]
; *Rohig (UK) Ltd v Rock Unique Ltd* [2011] EWCA Civ 18; [2011] 2 All E.R. (Comm) 1161 (freight forwarder: reasonable).

[Add at the end of fn.461]
; *Axa Sun Life Services Plc v Campbell Martin Ltd* [2011] EWCA Civ 133; [2011] 2 Lloyd's Rep. 1 (insurance representative: not reasonable); *Rohig (UK) Ltd v Rock Unique Ltd* [2011] EWCA Civ 18; [2011] 2 All E.R. (Comm) 1161 (freight forwarder: reasonable).

Clauses in consumer contracts or standard terms

13–095   *[Insert at the end of the penultimate sentence of fn.474]*
[. . .but reasonable]; *Axa Sun Life Services Plc v Campbell Martin Ltd* [2011] EWCA Civ 133; [2011] 2 Lloyd's Rep. 1 at [50] (applicability considered by Stanley Burnton L.J.). The *SAM Business Systems* case is reported at [2003] 1 All E.R. (Comm) 465.

Standard terms

13–096   *[Add at the end of fn.487]*
; *Yuanda (UK) Co Ltd v Ww Gear Construction Ltd* [2010] EWHC 720 (TCC); [2010] 1 C.L.C.491 at [23] *et seq.* (construction contract: but containing a useful discussion of the notion of standard terms).

Contracts to which the Act does not apply: international supply contracts

13–100   *[In line 1 of fn.504, replace "26–103" with "26–102"]*

[Add at the end of fn.504]
; *Air Transworld Ltd v Bombardier Inc* [2012] EWHC 243 (Comm); [2012] 1 Lloyd's Rep. 349 (containing much useful discussion).

Evasion of Act by choice of foreign law

13–102   *[Add at the end of fn.508]*
The section was recently found inapplicable in *Air Transworld Ltd v Bombardier Inc* [2012] EWHC 243 (Comm); [2012] 1 Lloyd's Rep. 349.

Liability in tort

13–107   *[Amend fn.531]*
Clerk and Lindsell on Torts (20th edn, 2010), paras 3–91 *et seq.*

13–108   *[Add new fn.544A after "excluded" in line 4 of p.738]*

544A See a useful discussion in *Clerk and Lindsell on Torts* (20th edn, 2010), para.8–125.

[Amend fn.544]
Titan Steel Wheels Ltd v Royal Bank of Scotland Plc [2011] 2 Lloyd's Rep. 92.

Part Five

CONSUMER PROTECTION

CHAPTER 14

CONSUMER PROTECTION

1. INTRODUCTION

Introduction

[*fn.3, line 8 after* "distance contracts" *insert*]   **14–001**
(repealed and replaced as from June 13, 2014 by Directive 2011/83/EU)

[*fn.3, line 19 delete* "a Proposal for a Directive . . . analysis of the proposal" *and insert*]
Directive 2011/83/EU on consumer rights [2011] OJ L 304/64, which will apply to contracts concluded after June 13, 2014 (art.28.2). In its original form the Directive was envisaged as being one which would lay down maximum and not only minimum rights: see COM (2008) 614/3 published on October 8, 2008. However, this approach was modified in important respects such that the principle of maximum harmonisation now has a more limited application. For a detailed analysis of the original proposal

2. RIGHTS UNDER THE CIVIL LAW

(a) *Rights of Buyer Against Seller*

Unordered goods

14–004   [*Add at the end of fn.11*]
See also Directive 2011/83/EU, art.27 (inertia selling).

[*Add after the first sentence of fn.14*]
Note that Directive 2005/29/EC, art.5.5, Annex I, point 29 designates inertia selling to consumers as a commercial practice which is in all circumstances considered unfair and is hence prohibited.

Late delivery

14–006   [*Add at the end of fn.25*]
In respect of contracts with consumers concluded after June 13, 2014 Directive 2011/83/EU will set out more prescriptive provisions covering late delivery: see arts 18 and 28.2.

Implied obligations as to quality, etc.: background and the EC Directive on consumer sales

14–008   [*fn.39, in the last sentence delete* "More recently the commission has" *and insert*]
The Commission had originally

[*Add at the end of fn.39*]
However, the proposal was not proceeded with and was replaced by limited reporting requirements: see Directive 2011/83/EU, art.33.

Satisfactory quality and fitness for purpose

14–010   [*fn.61, insert before last sentence*]
Note also that in respect of contracts with consumers concluded after June 13, 2014 the general position with respect to the passing of risk will be affected by Directive 2011/83/EU on consumer rights: see arts 20 and 28.2.

Compliance with the Directive: definitions

14–011   [*Add at the end of fn.65*]
No doubt, further changes will be required when implementing Directive 2011/83/EU, art.20.

Remedies for defective goods: rejection and damages

14–020   [*fn.101, line 2, delete* "is currently under discussion" *and insert*]
has been discussed

[Add at the end of fn.101]
However, in respect of such remedies in consumer sales the proposal was not carried forward to the resultant Directive 2011/83/EU, thus allowing the remedy of rejection to remain intact.

[Add at the end of fn.157] **14–028**
However, in respect of such remedies in consumer sales the proposal was not carried forward to the resultant Directive 2011/83/EU. For comparison of the remedies afforded by the proposed Directive and English law, see Naidoo [2011] J.B.L. 805.

(b) *Exemption Clauses and Unfair Contract Terms*

Unfair Terms in Consumer Contracts Regulations 1999

[fn.182, line 9, after "repealed and replaced" *add]* **14–031**
by one imposing maximum and not only minimum levels of protection

[Add at the end of fn.182]
However, the proposal was not proceeded with and was replaced by limited reporting requirements where more stringent provisions were imposed, in particular where such provisions "extend the unfairness assessment to individually negotiated contractual terms or to the adequacy of the price or remuneration; or contain lists of contractual terms which shall be considered as unfair": see Directive 2011/83/EU, art.32.

Scope of the Regulations

[Add at the end of fn.191] **14–032**
However, in *UK Housing Alliance Ltd v Francis* [2010] EWCA Civ 117; [2010] 3 All E.R. 519 the Court of Appeal held that the mere fact than a consumer had had the opportunity of considering and influencing the term did *not* mean that that term had been individually negotiated.

[Add at the end of fn.203] **14–035**
; Whittaker, 73 M.L.R. 106 (2010).

[Add at the end of fn.208]
For an application of this approach, see *OFT v Foxtons Ltd* [2009] EWHC 1681 (Ch); [2009] 29 E.G. 98 (C.S.) (Mann J.).

[Add at the end of fn.210]
Cf. *OFT v Ashbourne Management Services Ltd* [2011] EWHC 1237 (Ch) (Kitchen J.), holding that reg.6(2)(a) did not preclude an assessment as to the fairness of various terms in contracts for gym membership.

[fn.220, line 10, just before "See also" *insert]* **14–037**
; *Du Plessis v Fontgary Leisure Parks Ltd* [2012] EWCA 409 (term allowing owner and operator of a caravan site to increase fee charged to caravan owners to use pitches on site not "unfair").

(c)   *Miscellaneous Matters*

Doorstep sales

14–047   [*fn.286, delete the last sentence*]

[*fn.287, delete* "both cash and credit purchasers . . . affected by the need" *and insert*]
and other holiday accommodation contracts (whether involving cash or credit) the Timeshare, Holiday Products, Resale and Exchange Contracts Regulations 2010, SI 2010/2960 (as amended by SI 2011/1065) provide consumers with extensive protection covering such matters as requirements to provide information and rights of withdrawal. The Regulations have been enacted

14–048   [*Add at the end of fn.302*]
Note also that Directive 2011/83/EU [2011] OJ L304/64, arts 6 to 16, contains detailed provisions covering what it terms "off-premises contracts" which will apply to contracts concluded after June 13, 2014 (art.28.2). The Directive, which in this area is one of maximum and not only minimum harmonisation (art.4), repeals and replaces (art.31) Council Directive 1985/577/EEC [1985] OJ L372/31 and it may be assumed that amendments to English law will be required to implement it.

(f)   *Distance Selling*

The Distance Selling Regulations

14–058   [*Delete the last sentence of fn.340 and insert*]
However, the position in this respect will be changed with the implementation of Directive 2011/83/EU [2011] OJ L304/64, which will apply to contracts concluded after June 13, 2014 (art.28.2). The Directive, which in this area is one of maximum and not only minimum harmonisation, (art.4) repeals and replaces (art.31) Directive 97/7/EC and it may be assumed that amendments to English law will be required to implement it.

[*Add at the end of fn.341*]
and SI 2010/2960.

[*fn.351, delete* Timeshare Act 1992" *and insert*]
Timeshare, Holiday Products, Resale and Exchange Contracts Regulations 2010, SI 2010/2960.

Information to be provided

14–059   [*Add at the end of fn.360*]
Further guidance may be found by analogy with the more recent definition of "durable medium" in Directive 2011/83/EU, art.2.10, which states that it means "any instrument which enables the consumer or the trader to store information addressed personally to him in a way accessible for future reference for a period

of time adequate for the purposes of the information and which allows the unchanged reproduction of the information stored." Examples given in Recital 23 refer in particular to paper, USB sticks, CD-ROMs, DVDs, memory cards or the hard disks of computers as well as e-mails.

Manufacturer's tort liability at common law

[Add at the end of fn.414]   **14–065**
; *Divya v Toyo Tire and Rubber Co Ltd* [2011] EWHC 1993 (QB); [2011] All E.R. (D) 264 (July).

    (i)   *Rights of a User Who Did Not Buy the Product*

Remedies in tort

[fn.489, line 4, just before "cf." add]   **14–080**
Divya v Toyo Tire and Rubber Co Ltd [2011] EWHC 1993 (QB); [2011] All E.R. (D) 264 July.

    (j)   *Liability under Part I of the Consumer Protection Act 1987*

Background

[fn.515, line 15, delete "Unreported June 4, 2009" and insert]   **14–084**
[2009] E.C.R. I-4733, paras 24 and 25

[fn.515, line 17, Just before "For an assessment" add]
; *Centre Hospitalier Universitaire de Besancon v Thomas Dutrueux* (C-495/10) (Unreported December 21, 2011) (French law imposing liability without fault on public healthcare establishment permissible even though as a service provider it was not a "producer" (art.3) of the heated mattress which caused burns following the failure of the temperature-control mechanism during surgery). In both cases the situation simply fell outside the scope of the Directive.

Products within the scope of the Act

[Insert before the last case reference in fn.526]   **14–086**
Kingsway Hall Hotel Ltd v Red Sky IT (Hounslow) Ltd [2010] EWHC 965 (TCC); (2010) 26 Const. L.J. 542.

3.   THE CONSUMER'S REMEDIES

Class and group actions

[Add at the end of fn.633]   **14–107**
; Hodges [2010] C.J.Q, 370; Wagner, 127 L.Q.R. 55 (2011); Mulheron 127 L.Q.R. 288 (2011).

14–108   [*fn.638, delete* "For" *and insert*]
However, r.19.6 continues to make provision for cases involving representative parties with the "same interest". For a modern example of a case involving allegations of price fixing where the claimant did not have the "same interest" as those it sought to represent, see *Emerald Supplies Ltd v British Airways Plc* [2010] EWCA Civ 1284; [2011] Ch. 345. See, generally, Zuckerman, *Civil Procedure— Principles of Practice* (2nd edn) and for

4. CRIMINAL LAW

The Food Safety Act 1990

14–114   [*fn.684, line 1, after* "(SI 2004/3279)" *add*]
, as amended by SI 2005/2626)

The Weights and Measures Act 1985

14–115   [*line 13, after* "an inspector" *add*]
or approved verifier

[*line 26, delete* "and s.29 . . . quantity thereof"]

Safety regulations and the general safety requirement

14–119   [*fn.729, last line, delete* "2007 (SI 2007/2790) as amended" *and insert*]
2010 (SI 2010/2225)

[*fn.734, delete* "SI 2006/2739 . . . SI 2008 2852" *and insert*]
SI 2012/632

[*Amend fn.737*]
SI 1987/1337

[*Add at the end of fn.738*]
and SI 2010/2205

[*fn.742, delete* "and SI 2010/864" *and insert*]
(as amended in both cases by SI 2011/1256 and SI 2012/677); also, SI 2010/864

[*Add at the end of fn.746*]
, as amended by SI 2011/2157

[*Amend fn.753*]
SI 2011/1881

[*Add at the end of fn.757*]
, SI 2010/1927, SI 2011/881 and SI 2011/3037

[*Amend fn. 759*]
SI 2004/1836, as amended by SI 2004/3262 and SI 2010/1554. See also
Fireworks Act 2003.

[*Add at the end of fn. 761*]
, SI 2005/894, SI 2005/1806, SI 2006/1492, SI 2009/1504 and SI 2011/988.

[*Add at the end of fn. 762*]
, as amended by SI 2011/1881

[*fn. 766, just before* "SI 2004/568" *insert*]
SI 2001/1426,

[*Add at the end of fn. 768*]
and SI 2010/1881

Consumer Protection from Unfair Trading Regulations 2008

[*fn. 842, line 4, delete* "Unreported January 14, 2010 ECJ" *and insert*]   **14–129**
[2011] 1 All E.R. (EC) 338 (ECJ); *Media Print Zeitungs-und Zeitschriftenverlag
GmbH & Co KG v Osterreich-Zeitungsverlag-Gmbh* (C-540/08) [2011] 2 All E.R.
(Comm) 697 ECJ.

Scope of the Regulations

[*Line 11, after* "(reg.2(1))" *insert new fn. 845A*]   **14–130**

845A In *R. (on the application of Surrey Trading Standards) v Scottish & Southern
Energy Plc* [2012] EWCA Crim 539 it was held that a non-trading entity such as
a holding company could be a "trader" for the purposes of the Regulations even
though it did not did not directly supply the product (electricity) which was the
subject of the allegedly misleading commercial practice.

Practices considered unfair in all circumstances

[*Add at the end of fn. 873*]   **14–133**
See also para.31 (creating a false impression that the consumer has already
won, or will win, a prize) which was held to have been contravened in *OFT v
Purely Creative Ltd* [2011] EWHC 106 (Ch); [2011] E.C.C.20 (Briggs J.: considering also regs 3, 5 and 6 and, in particular, the phrases "average consumer",
"transactional decision" and "material information"). The interpretation of Annex
I, para.31 was subsequently referred to the ECJ: see *Purely Creative Ltd v OFT*
[2011] EWCA Civ 920; [2012] 1 C.M.L.R. 21.

Offences, defences, penalties and enforcement

[*Add at the end of the text*]   **14–137**
However, neither the Regulations nor the Directive currently make provision
for a civil remedy to compensate consumers who have suffered loss as a result of
an unfair commercial practice involving misleading or aggressive conduct on the

part of a trader, although provision to compensate such losses may of course be made under some other recognised head, for example, misrepresentation. The Law Commission and the Scottish Law Commission have recommended that legislation be introduced to provide redress to consumers where such conduct is present. The proposed reform is, however, relatively limited and stops short of recommending an automatic right of redress where there has been a breach of the Regulations.[901A]

[901A] See *Consumer Redress for Misleading and Aggressive Practices* (Law Com No 332, Scot Law Com No 226; Cm 8323, March 2012).

5. ADMINISTRATIVE PROTECTION

The definitions of "consumer"

14–145   [*fn.945, after* "SI 2006/3363" *delete* "regs 4 and 5)" *and insert*]
, regs 3, 4 and 5) and SI 2011/1043, art.4(1).

Domestic infringements

14–146   [*fn.947, after* "as amended by" *delete* "SI 2008/1277 Sch.2 para.102 Sch.4 Pt 2" *and insert*]
SI 2008/1277, reg.30(1), (3), Sch.2, para.102, Sch.4 Pt 2, SI 2010/1554, SI 2010/2960 and SI 2011/1265.

Community infringements

14–147   [*fn.953, line 2, delete* "SI 2006/3372 art.2(2) and Sch."]

[*fn.953, delete the last sentence and insert*]
, SI 2010/1010 reg.69, SI 2010/2960, reg.36, Sch.6 and 8 and SI 2011/1208, reg.17.

[*fn.954, delete* "and (iii) amending . . . (SI 2010/1010) reg.46." *and insert*]
More recently, the Consumer Credit (EU Directive) Regulations 2010, SI 2010/1010, reg.46, repealed the entry for para.3 and inserted a new entry, para.9D (consumer credit) and the Timeshare, Holiday Products, Resale and Exchange Contracts Regulations 2010, SI 2010/2960, reg.36, Sch.6 deleted para.6 and added para.9E.

[*fn.957, delete* "See Directive 1987/102 . . . OJ L133/66" *and insert*]
See Directive 2008/48 [2008] OJ L133/66

[*Delete existing text in fn.960 and insert*]
See Directive 2008/122 [2008] OJ L33/10 on timeshare and related contracts and the corresponding provisions in the Timeshare, Holiday Products, Resale and Exchange Contracts Regulations 2010, SI 2010/2960.

[*Main text, third line from the bottom, after* "timeshares" *add*]
and similar arrangements

[*Add at the end of fn.984*]   **14–151**
For an example of a case in which alternative sources were under considera-
tion, see *OFT v Ashbourne Management Services Ltd* [2011] EHC 1237 (Ch)
(Kitchen J.).

Regulatory Enforcement and Sanctions Act 2008

[*Renumber fn.1002 as*]   **14–155**
1002–1003

6. INDIRECT PROTECTION

Advertising control

[*Delete second sentence including footnote, and first word of third sentence,*   **14–156**
and insert]
They

7. CONSUMER CREDIT TRANSACTIONS

Consumer Credit Act 1974

[*fn.1022, line 4, after* "regs 64 to 67." *add*]   **14–158**
Subsequent amendments have been introduced by SI 2010/1969, regs 20
and 21.

[*fn.1027, line 2, after* "the creditor" *add*]
or owner

Implementing Directive 2008/48

[*All Regulations mentioned as coming into force on February 1, 2011 are now*   **14–159**
in force]

[*Add at the end of fn.1029*]
, since amended by SI 2010/1969 and SI 2011/11.

[*Add at the end of fn.1030*]
, with more recent amendments, including the introduction of a new reg.101A,
being introduced by SI 2010/1969, regs 5 and 28 to 30.

[*Add at the end of fn.1031*]
, since amended by SI 2011/11.

[Delete the text in fn.1035 and insert]
Originally SI 2010/1012, but since revoked and replaced by SI 2010/1970.

[fn.1036, delete "1012" and insert]
1970

[Add at the end of fn.1038]
with the wording being subsequently corrected by SI 2010/1969, reg.23.

[Add at the end of fn.1039]
, since amended by SI 2010/1969 and SI 2011/11.

[fn.1042, delete first sentence and insert]
See SI 2010/1010, reg.75, as amended by SI 2010/1969, reg.24; SI 2010/1013, reg.2, as amended by SI 2010/1969, reg.33.

[Add at the end of fn.1043]
, as amended by SI 2010/1969.

[fn.1044, add after "reg.1(2)(a)"]
, as amended by SI 2010/1969, reg.42.

[fn.1046, line 1, after "reg.2" add]
(2)

14–160   *[fn.1050, after the first sentence, add]*
Section 16B has been amended by the Energy Act 2011, s.25, which makes provision for "green deal plans".

14–161   *[Add at the end of fn.1054]*
For transitional provisions and savings, see SI 2010/1010, regs 100(1), 101, 101A (as inserted by SI 2010/1969, regs 4, 30).

[Add at the end of fn.1056]
See also SI 2007/1168. Article 6 and Sch.3, which makes provision for the form and content of declarations for exemption relating to businesses.

[Insert new para.14–161A]

14–161A   The general level of complexity is increased by the fact that the 2006 Act is an amending, rather than a consolidating, measure and by the principal supporting Regulations[1057A] having been extensively amended[1057B] or, in one case, having been revoked and replaced to correct drafting errors.[1057C]

[1057A] That is, SI 2010/1010, SI 2010/1011, SI 2010/1012, SI 2010/1013 and SI 2010/2014.
[1057B] Notably, by the Consumer Credit (Amendment) Regulations 2010, SI 2010/1969 and the Consumer Credit (Amendment) Regulations 2011, SI 2011/11.
[1057C] The original Consumer Credit (Advertisements) Regulations 2010, SI 2010/1012 were revoked and replaced by SI 2010/1970.

Outline of control

[*fn.1058, line 1, after* "reg.7" *add*]   **14–162**
with transitional provisions and savings: see SI 2010/1969, regs 4, 30

[*fn.1058, line 4, after* "51 to 56" *add*]
, SI 2010/1969, reg.2.

[*fn.1058, line 6, after* "2011" *add*]
and which have since been amended by SI 2010/1969, regs 41 to 46. For a case
in which the requirements of s.61 and of the Consumer Credit (Agreements)
Regulations 1983 were held to have been satisfied, see *Brophy v HFC Bank* [2011]
EWCA Civ 67; [2011] E.C.C. 14. Cf. *Harrison v Link Financial Ltd* [2011] E.C.C.
26 (non-compliance of creditor with ss.61(1) and 78(1)).

[*fn.1058, line 8, after* "73 to 76" *add*]
and subsequently by SI 2010/ 1969, regs 24 and 25.

[*fn.1058, line 10, after* "(SI 2010/1013)" *add*]
, as amended by SI 2010/1969, regs 31 to 40

[*fn.1058, line 11, delete* "3 and 4" *and insert*]
regs 2 to 4 (as amended by SI 2010/1969, regs 4, 6)

[*Add at the end of fn.1058*]
For transitional provisions and savings, see SI 2010/1010, regs 100(1), 101,
101A, (as inserted by SI 2010/1969, regs 4, 30).

[*fn.1061, line 4, after* "regs 8 and 9" *delete the semi-colon and add*]
. For transitional provisions and savings, see SI 2010/1010, regs 100(1), 101
and 101A (as inserted by SI 2010/1969, regs 4, 29, 30). See

[*Add at the end of fn.1061*]
A further amendment was introduced by SI 2010/1969, reg.18.

[*fn.1062, add after* "SI 2010/1010 reg.13"]
and amended by SI 2010/1969, regs 4, 8

[*fn.1063, delete the first sentence and insert*]
1974 Act ss.76, 77, 77A, 77B, 78 (matters arising during currency of agreement) and (in relation to default and termination) 87, 98, 98A.

[*fn.1063, line 6, after* "amend s.88" *add*]
Sections 86B and 86C have been variously amended by SI 2008/2826.

[*fn.1063, line 15, delete* "and SI 2008/2826"]

[*fn.1065, line 4, after* "regs 59 to 62" *add*]
with reg.60 having been further amended by SI 2010/1969, reg.19

[*fn.1065, line 5/6, after* "regs 77 to 84" *add*]
with reg.78 having been further amended by SI 2010/1969, reg.26.

[*Add at the end of fn.1068*]
, as amended by Consumer Credit Act 2006, s.16(1).

[*fn.1071, line 4, after* "(Flaux J.)." *add*]
In relation to s.78(1) (duty to give information to debtor on request under a running account agreement), see *Phoenix Recoveries (UK) Ltd v Kotecha* [2011] EWCA Civ 105; [2011] E.C.C. 13 (no entitlement to enforce agreement while failure of creditor to give information continues: s.78(6)(a)); also, *Harrison v Link Financial Ltd* [2011] E.C.C. 26 (non-compliance of creditor with ss.61(1) and 78(1)).

[*fn.1072, line 1, after* "new s.77A" *add*]
(since amended by SI 2008/2826, art.4, SI 2010/1010, reg.23 and Energy Act 2011, s.27)

Licensing

14–163   [*fn.1075, delete* "s.31 Sch.3 para.15(3)" *and insert*]
ss.19, 23, 31

[*fn.1076, line 1, delete* "1976" *and insert*]
1974

[*fn.1076, delete the last sentence*]

[*fn.1077, delete* "s.31 Sch.3 para.15(3)" *and insert*]
ss.19, 31

[*fn.1079, delete* "; see also . . . reg.38(3)"]

[*Add at the end of fn.1082*]
See also SI 2010/1010, reg.101A (as inserted by SI 2010/1969, regs 4, 30).

Hire-purchase and conditional sale

14–164   [*Add at the end of fn.1085*]
, as amended by Consumer Credit Act 2006, s.5(2)(a).

[*fn.1086, delete* "Wilson v Robertsons . . . W.L.R. 1248" *and insert*]
Southern Pacific Personal Loans Ltd v Walker [2010] UKSC 3; [2010] 1 W.L.R. 1819.

Credit-sale

14–165   [*Add at the end of fn.1093*]
, as amended by Consumer Credit Act, 2006, s.5(2)(a).

[*Add at the end of fn.1094*]
, as amended by Consumer Credit Act, 2006, s.5(2)(a).

[*Line 9, just before fn.1096, insert*]
and the credit is provided without interest and without any other charges.

[*fn.1096, delete* "reg.66(a) . . . other charges"." *and insert*]
regs 64, 66(b).

[*Line 11, delete* "(*e.g.* monthly) . . . single payment" *and insert*]
not exceeding three months, which requires that the number of payments to be made by the debtor in repayment of the whole amount of the credit provided in each such period shall not exceed one and in relation to which no or insignificant charges are payable for the credit.

[*fn.1097, delete* "reg.66(b) . . . the credit"." *and insert*]
regs 64, 66(b).

Credit cards, etc

[*fn.1098, after* "art.3(1)(a)(ii)" *insert*]   **14–166**
, as substituted by the Consumer Credit (EU Directive) Regulations 2010 (SI 2010/1010), regs 64, 66(a)

[*fn.1101, delete* "(a), (b)"]

[*Add at the end of fn.1102*]
, as amended by Consumer Credit Act, 2006, s.5(2)(a).

[*Add at the end of fn.1103*]
, as amended by SI 2010/1010, regs 2, 45.

[*fn.1105, line 3, delete* "3236 art.4" *and insert*]
2619, reg.2

[*Delete the text in fn.1107 and insert*]
Payment Services Regulations 2009 (SI 2009/209) regs 60, 61, 62, especially 62(3)(c) and (4).

Protection of the Act

[*fn.1111, line 3, after* "SI 1999/3177" *insert*]   **14–167**
and SI 2010/1010

[*fn.1111, line 4, after* "February 1, 2011" *add*]
and which have since been amended by SI 2011/11;

[*fn.1111, line 6, after* "2008/1277" *add*]
, SI 2010/1010, SI 2010/1969 and SI 2011/11

[*fn.1111, line 7, amend* "SI 2010/1012" *to*]
SI 2010/1970

14–168   [*fn.1113, line 1, delete* "See 1974 Act" *and insert*]
See 2006 Act

[*Add at the end of fn.1113*]
For consideration of the transitional provisions introduced by s.69 and Sch.3 to the 2006 Act, see *Barnes v Black Horse Ltd* [2011] EWHC 1416 (QB); [2011] 2 All E.R. (Comm) 1130.

[*Add at the end of fn.1115*]
Harrison v Black Horse Ltd [2010] EWHC 3152 (QB); [2011] Lloyd's Rep. I.R. 455, [50] (Judge Waksman, QC: interference with decision of first instance judge generally inappropriate unless it proceeded upon failure to consider an obviously relevant factor, consideration of an obviously irrelevant one or an erroneous view of law).

14–171   [*fn.1130, line 2, add after* "£30,000."]
For discussion of problems associated with this lower limit, especially in the context of internet sales, see Adams [2011] J.B.L. 271.

[*fn.1130, line 4, add after* "reg.25"]
and amended by SI 2010/1969, regs 4, 11

[*Add at the end of fn.1130*]
For transitional provisions and savings which apply to ss.75 and 75A, see SI 2010/1010, regs 100(1), 101 and 101A (as inserted by SI 2010/1969, regs 4, 30).

[*Add at the end of fn.1132*]
For criticism of the role of s.75 in credit card transactions, see Bisping [2011] J.B.L. 457.

Advertisements and enforcement

14–172   [*fn.1137, line 1, add after* "s.43 has been amended"]
inter alia

[*fn.1138, line 3, delete* "credit consumer" *and insert*]
regulated consumer credit

[*fn.1138, line 4, after* "reg.72" *insert*]
, as amended by SI 2010/1969, reg.23

[*fn.1139, amend* "SI 2010/1012" *to*]
SI 2010/1970

[*Add at the end of fn.1139*]
These Regulations revoked and replaced the Consumer Credit (Advertisement) Regulations 2010, SI 2010/1012.

Part Six

REMEDIES

CHAPTER 15

THE SELLER'S REMEDIES AFFECTING THE GOODS

2.   LIEN

(b)   *When the Lien Arises*

Possession of the goods

[Add at the end of fn.239]   **15–038**
and see *Re Redfern Resources Ltd* [2011] BCSC 711 (Can) where the Court
held that the seller could not rely on its lien because possession of the goods had
passed to the buyer's agent (at [39]).

3.   STOPPAGE IN TRANSIT

(b)   *Duration of Transit*

Acknowledgment to the buyer

15–077   [*Add at the end of fn.502*]
And see *Re Redfern Resources Ltd* [2011] BCSC 771 (Can) where the Court
held that the transit was at an end (at [42]), when the equipment was stored by the
carrier as the agent of the buyer and the buyer was billed for storage.

5.   RESALE

(a)   *Introduction*

Wrongful resale

15–104   [*fn.704, after the* Goff and Jones *reference, insert*]
(There is no corresponding material in Goff and Jones, *The Law of Unjust
Enrichment* (8th edn).)

Agency of necessity

15–106   [*Amend fn.716*]
Goff and Jones, *The Law of Unjust Enrichment* (8th edn), paras 18–50 *et seq.*

(b)   *Termination of Contract upon Buyer's Repudiation or Breach*

Specific restitution of the goods

15–116   [*fn.798, after the Goff and Jones reference, insert*]
(There is no corresponding material in Goff and Jones, *The Law of Unjust
Enrichment* (8th edn).)

Revesting of property in other circumstances

15–118   [*fn.820, add after* "Infants Relief Act 1874"]
(subsequently repealed by the Minors' Contracts Act 1987)

(f)   *Forfeiture of Deposits or Other Prepayments*

Forfeiture of deposits

15–132   [*Add at the end of fn.912*]
The usual rule is that time for compliance is strict and of the essence:
Samarenkov Dawn Hill House Ltd [2011] EWCA Civ 1445 at [53], [54] *per*
Etherton L.J.; and [61] *per* Rix L.J.

CHAPTER 16

OTHER REMEDIES OF THE SELLER

1. THE CLAIM FOR THE PRICE

(d) *Entitlement to Sue for the Price*

(i) *Where the Property has Passed to the Buyer*

Action for price when property has passed

[Add at the end of fn.155]   **16–021**
In *Abraaj Investment Management Ltd v Bregawn Jersey Ltd* [2010] EWHC 630 (Comm) at [19], Teare J. held that unless otherwise agreed, delivery of the goods and payment of the price are concurrent conditions so that no claim for the price could be maintained in the absence of delivery: "Since Abraaj is not able to deliver the goods and has not offered to do so, it cannot establish a right to the price." See further para.16–016 above and para.19–231 below.

2. GENERAL RULES ON DAMAGES

(c) *Remoteness of Damage and Causation*

Remoteness of damage

16–043   [*Add at the end of fn.348*]
In *MFM Restaurants Pte Ltd v Fish & Co Restaurants Pte Ltd* [2010] SGCA 36, (not a sale of goods case) the Singapore Court of Appeal considered the speeches in *The Achilleas (supra)* at length and considered the extent to which assumption of responsibility was a distinct requirement or merely an aspect of the existing doctrine of remoteness. At [103] of the opinion the Court suggests that the first limb in *Hadley v Baxendale* (1854) 9 Ex. 341 embodies an implied under-taking or assumption of responsibility and (at [107] and [115]) that the criterion of knowledge in the second limb in *Hadley v Baxendale* furnishes the basis on which to premise the existence of an implied obligation or assumption of responsibility by the defendant. It then suggests (at [109]) that the two limbs in *Hadley v Baxendale* are in substance what the parties would have agreed to had they thought about a situation in which the contract was breached. Accordingly an assumption of responsibility was an aspect of the existing doctrine and it followed that the two limbs set out in *Hadley v Baxendale* continue to be the governing principles in relation to the doctrine of remoteness.

[*fn.350, add after quotation from* Sylvia Shipping]
and *Borealis AB v Geogas Trading SA* [2010] EWHC 2789 (Comm); [2011] 1 Lloyd's Rep. 482 at [48].

The degree of probability

16–044   [*Add at the end of fn.359*]
See *Hi-Lite Electrical Limited v Wolseley UK Limited* [2011] EWHC 2153, at [215]: "The correct question . . . is whether at the time of the contract, a fire was not unlikely to result from a manufacturing defect in the cable or that there was a serious possibility of loss by fire arising from that manufacturing defect." See below at para.17–072 fn.561.

Causation

16–049   [*Add at the beginning of fn.398*]
The legal burden of proof rests throughout on the claimant to prove that the defendant's breach caused its loss: see *Borealis AB v Geogas Trading SA* [2010] EWHC 2789 (Comm); [2011] 1 Lloyd's Rep. 482 at [43].

[*Add at the end of fn.399*]
The approach to the question must always be that the claimant must prove the cause of the damage on the balance of probabilities: See *Hi-Lite Electrical Ltd v Wolseley UK Ltd* [2011] EWHC 2153 (TCC) at [131]–[135]. In that case the trial Judge found that the claimant which was seeking compensation for damage to its

hair salon caused by a fire had not established that the cause of the fire was a manufacturing defect in an electrical pump acquired from the seller. He found that on the balance of probabilities the likely cause was a staff member cutting the cable whilst cleaning away hair and gunk which had accumulated in the pump and over the cable.

[Add at the end of fn.404]
In *Borealis AB v Geogas Trading SA* [2010] EWHC 2789 (Comm) at [43]–[47], Gross L.J. stated that the following principles can be derived from previous decisions on causation:

(1)   Although an evidential burden rests on the defendant insofar as it contends that there was a break in the chain of causation, the legal burden of proof rests throughout on the claimant to prove that the defendant's breach of contract caused its loss.

(2)   In order to comprise a *novus actus interveniens*, so breaking the chain of causation, the conduct of the claimant "must constitute an event of such impact that it 'obliterates' the wrongdoing . . ." of the defendant. For there to be a break in the chain of causation, the true cause of the loss must be the conduct of the claimant rather than the breach of contract on the part of the defendant; if the breach of contract by the defendant and the claimant's subsequent conduct are concurrent causes, it must be unlikely that the chain of causation will be broken. In circumstances where the defendant's breach of contract remains an effective cause of the loss, at least ordinarily, the chain of causation will not be broken.

(3)   It is difficult to conceive that anything less than unreasonable conduct on the part of the claimant would be capable of breaking the chain of causation. It is, however, also plain that mere unreasonable conduct on a claimant's part will not necessarily do so.

(4)   The claimant's state of knowledge at the time of and following the defendant's breach of contract is likely to be a factor of very great significance.

(5)   That the question of whether there has been a break in the chain of causation is fact sensitive, involving as it does a practical inquiry into the circumstances of the defendant's breach of contract and the claimant's subsequent conduct.

[Add at the end of fn.408]
; and see *Hi-Lite Electrical Ltd v Wolseley UK Ltd* [2011] EWHC 2153 (TCC) at [202]–[207]. In that case it had been found that a fire which had damaged the claimant's hair dressing salon had on the balance of probabilities been caused by acts of the claimant's staff cutting a cable whilst cleaning away hair and gunk which had accumulated over the cable and not by a manufacturing defect in the goods supplied by the seller (an electrical pump). The Judge nevertheless went on to consider what the position would have been had he found otherwise and had found there had been a manufacturing defect in the pump supplied by the seller. The seller had submitted that even in that event the seller should not be held responsible for the damage as the buyer should have fitted a safety device (an

RCD) to protect the pump circuit in accordance with the manufacturer's instructions. The existence of an RCD would have prevented the fire. The Judge said (at [207]) that the failure to fit the RCD would not have broken the chain of causation: "whilst the existence of the RCD would have prevented the fire, I do not consider that the failure to fit the RCD could be said to deprive any breach by Wolseley which caused the fire of its causative potency so that it would still remain an effective cause . . . the fact that there are two causes does not, in law, deprive one cause of its causative effect."

Loss of chance

16–050   *[Add at the end of fn.410]*
The rationale of the loss of chance doctrine is to permit recovery to a claimant who by reason of uncertainty would otherwise be unable to prove causation to the standard of the balance of probabilities. It is not to deny recovery to a claimant who successfully meets that burden. It follows that where a claimant can establish causation on a balance of probabilities there is no relevant uncertainty as to causation and no need to reduce damages on the basis of a loss of chance: see *Aercap Partners 1 Ltd v Avia Asset Management Ltd* [2010] EWHC 2431 (Comm) at [76].

Contributory negligence

16–051   *[Add at the end of fn.422]*
And see *Hi-Lite Electrical Ltd v Wolseley UK Ltd* [2011] EWHC 2153 (TCC) at [234] ("The provisions of s.14(2) are strict liability provisions and . . . a party liable in relation to such a contractual duty cannot reduce that liability by an apportionment to take account of the negligence of the other party.")

(d)   *Mitigation of Damage*

No recovery for loss which should have been avoided

16–052   *[fn.431, insert after "at p.506"]*
; *Borealis AB v Geogas Trading SA* [2010] EWHC 2789 (Comm); [2011] 1 Lloyd's Rep. 482 at [50]

Recovery of loss or expense incurred while attempting to mitigate

16–058   *[Add at the end of fn.470]*
In *Choil Trading SA v Sahara Energy Resources Ltd* [2010] EWHC 374 (Comm) at [161], Christopher Clarke J. allowed the buyer to recover losses incurred under hedge contracts as a reasonable attempt at mitigation when defective goods were supplied to the buyer, the buyer had on-sold the goods to an on-buyer and the goods had been rejected by the on-buyer because of their defective quality. The Judge said that in principle there is no sensible or commercial reason why the Court should not take into account the costs of the hedging instruments: "In the present case the effect of *Choil* being left long in naptha was to

expose it to the risk of severe losses if the market dropped. It was reasonable for it to protect itself against those losses by hedging in the way that it did." There was evidence that the counterparty would also have hedged against such losses and that it was reasonable for it to have done so ([156]).

3.   THE SELLER'S CLAIM FOR DAMAGES

(a)   *Damages for Non-acceptance*

Normal measure of damages for non-acceptance

[*Add at the end of fn.499*] 16–061
The normal measure of damages was awarded in *McCandless Aircraft LC v Payne* [2010] EWHC 1835 (QB) at [207] (seller agreed to sell helicopter to buyer; helicopter resold when not accepted by buyer; claim for difference between contract price and resale price awarded under s.50).

(b)   *An Available Market*

The meaning of "available market"

[*Add at the end of fn.543*] 16–066
And see *Aercap Partners 1 Ltd v Avia Asset Management Ltd* [2010] EWHC 2431 (Comm) at [107] ("If the goods are offered for sale and there is no buyer at a fair price, it is difficult to conclude that there was an available market at the time in question").

Resale at a price lower or higher than the market or current price

[*Add at the end of fn.613*] 16–075
And see *Aercap Partners 1 Ltd v Avia Asset Management AB* [2010] EWHC 2431 at [108] (where there is an available market the market price must generally be taken when assessing the seller's damages—rather than any price the seller might have obtained on a resale, if above or below the market price).

(d)   *Anticipatory Breach*

Acceptance of the buyer's anticipatory repudiation

[*Add at the end of fn.647*] 16–081
and *Golden Strait Corp v Nippon Yusen Kubishika Kaisha* [2007] UKHL 12 at [17] *per* Lord Bingham, and at [34], *per* Lord Scott ("even here some period must usually be allowed to enable the necessary arrangements for the substitute sale or purchase to be made . . . The relevant market price for the purpose of assessing the quantum of the recoverable loss will be the market price at the expiration of that period"); [2007] 2 A.C. 353.

(f) *Consequential Losses and Expenses*

Incidental losses and expenses

16–086   [*Add at the end of fn.680*]
In *McCandless Aircraft LC v Payne and Eminence Aviation Limited* [2010] EWHC 1835 (QB) at [208] the claimant seller was awarded interest on a bank loan which it had utilised to fund the purchase by it of a helicopter which it then on-sold to the defendant buyer. The buyer had agreed in the sale and purchase agreement to assume liability for the seller's bank charges from the time of the purchase of the helicopter by the seller to the date of payment by the buyer.

4.   MISCELLANEOUS REMEDIES

Declarations

16–092   [*Delete text in existing fn.719 and insert*]
Polenghi Bros v Dried Milk Co Ltd (1904) 10 Com. Cas. 42 (below, paras 19–230 to 19–232). See above at para.16–016. The Court has a discretion to make a negative declaration, *e.g.* to the effect that the claimant is not liable to the defendant in respect of a certain matter: *Messier-Dowty Ltd v Sabena SA* [2000] 1 WLR 2040 (CA).

Thank you for purchasing 1st supplement to the 8th edition of Benjamin's Sale of Goods

 ## Don't miss important updates

So that you have all the latest information, **Benjamin's Sale of Goods** is supplemented regularly. Sign up today for a Standing Order to ensure you receive the updating supplements as soon as they publish. Setting up a Standing Order with Sweet & Maxwell is hassle-free, simply tick, complete and return this FREEPOST card and we'll do the rest.

You may cancel your Standing Order at any time by writing to us at Sweet & Maxwell, PO Box 2000, Andover, SP10 9AH stating the Standing Order you wish to cancel.

Alternatively, if you have purchased your copy of **Benjamin's Sale of Goods** from a bookshop or other trade supplier, please ask your supplier to ensure that you are registered to receive the new supplements.

All goods are subject to our 30 day Satisfaction Guarantee (applicable to EU customers only).

Yes, please send me new supplements of the 8th edition of **Benjamin's Sale of Goods** to be invoiced on publication, until I cancel the standing order in writing.

☐ All new supplements

Title .... Name ....

Organisation ....

Job title ....

Address ....

Postcode ....

Telephone ....

Email ....

S&M account number (if known) ....

PO number ....

All orders are accepted subject to the terms of this order form and our Terms of Trading. (see www.sweetandmaxwell.co.uk). By submitting this order form I confirm that I accept these terms and I am authorised to sign on behalf of the customer.

Signed .... Job Title ....

Print Name .... Date ....

UK VAT Number: GB 900 5487 43. Irish VAT Number: IE 9513874E. For customers in an EU member state (except UK & Ireland) please supply your VAT Number. VAT No [   ]

(BC007) V9 (04.2012) / KG

Delivery charges are not made for titles supplied to mainland UK. Non-mainland UK please add £4/€5 per delivery. Europe - please add £10/€13 for first item, £2.50/€3 for each additional item. Rest of World - please add £30/€38 for first item, £15/€19 for each additional item. For deliveries outside Europe please add £30/€42 for first item, £15/€21 for each additional item.

Goods will normally be dispatched within 3-5 working days of availability. The price charged to customers, irrespective of any prices quoted, will be the price specified in our price list current at the time of dispatch of the goods, as published on our website, unless the order is subject to a specific offer or discount in which case special terms may apply.

UK VAT is charged on all applicable sales at the prevailing rate except in the case of sales to Ireland where Irish VAT will be charged at the prevailing rate. Customers outside the EU will not be charged UK VAT.

Thomson Reuters (Professional) UK Limited – Legal Business (Company No. 1679046). 100 Avenue Road, Swiss Cottage, London NW3 3PF. Registered in England and Wales. Registered office: Aldgate House, 33 Aldgate High Street, London EC3N 1DL. Trades using various trading names, a list of which is posted on its website at sweetandmaxwell.co.uk

"Thomson Reuters" and the Thomson Reuters logo are trademarks of Thomson Reuters and its affiliated companies.

SWEET & MAXWELL

 THOMSON REUTERS

SWEET & MAXWELL

FREEPOST

PO BOX 2000

ANDOVER

SP10 9AH

UNITED KINGDOM

CHAPTER 17

THE REMEDIES OF THE BUYER

1. Damages for Non-Delivery

(b)   *An Available Market*

(iii)   *Anticipatory Repudiation*

Acceptance of the seller's anticipatory repudiation

17–014   [*Add at the end of fn.108*]
And see *Glencore Energy UK Ltd v Transworld Oil Ltd* [2010] EWHC 141 (Comm) at [67] ("in a case of anticipatory breach . . . the relevant date to take (subject to the rules on mitigation) is the due date for delivery, alternatively the date when the goods ought reasonably to have been delivered, not the date of the repudiation or the buyer's acceptance of it.")

The rules on mitigation

17–015   [*fn.112, add after* "at p.1140)"]
; *Glencore Energy UK Ltd v Transworld Oil Ltd* [2010] EWHC 141 (Comm) at [78] (buyer accepted seller's repudiation and closed out its hedge contracts thereby reducing its losses: held that "since the closing out on early termination established a lower loss than would otherwise have been incurred that has to be taken into account when determining recoverable loss.")

(d)   *Resale by the Buyer*

Relevance of sub-contracts

17–028   [*Add at the end of fn.203*]
And see *Choil Trading SA v Sahara Energy Resources Ltd* [2010] EWHC 374 (Comm) at [128]–[130] where it was held that since Choil was buying for resale generally, it could be contemplated that on breach it would go out into the market and buy substitute goods, so that damages were not to be calculated by reference to the prices at which it had resold the goods to on-buyers. The damages awarded to the buyers were not however an exact application of s.53(3) since the award did not involve taking the market value of the goods at the place and time of delivery: see *infra* para.17–054 at fn.416.

3.   Damages for Defective Quality

(b)   *Diminution in Value*

The relevant time for ascertaining values

17–054   [*Add at the end of fn.416*]

And see *Choil Trading SA v Sahara Energy Resources Ltd* [2010] EWHC 374 (Comm) at [116]–[118] and [131] where the Court held that the damages should be assessed not at the time of delivery to the buyer (August 13) but at the time that the goods were rejected after tests carried out on board the vessel revealed that the goods were contaminated (August 28). The goods had been delivered to the buyer on August 13 but the test results had become available on August 27 and the rejection occurred on August 28.

(c)   *Losses other than Diminution in Value*

(iii)   *Loss of Profit*

Loss of general custom (or of "repeat orders")

[Add at the end of fn.535]   **17–069**
In *Foaminol Laboratories Ltd v British Artid Plastics Ltd* [1941] 2 All E.R. 393, it was said that a buyer could recover damages for a loss of goodwill resulting from a breach of contract where the buyer could establish with sufficient certainty the occurrence of pecuniary loss and that such pecuniary loss was within the contemplation of the defaulting party when the contract was made (*ibid.*, at 400c). In *Tullis Russell Papermakers Ltd v Inveresk Limited* [2010] CSOH 148 (not a sale of goods case) the pursuer was successful in establishing the occurrence of pecuniary losses arising by virtue of a loss of general custom caused by the defendant's supply of defective product to the pursuer's customers on the basis of expert evidence which assessed the actual purchases made by customers and the likely purchases that would have been made but for the breach.

In that case the defendant had undertaken as part of the sale of a business division to the pursuer to continue manufacturing certain products for a period of five months and to maintain existing levels of customer service. The defendant also agreed to meet agreed quality standards in producing the further products to the pursuer's customers. There were material breaches of these obligations: defective product was supplied to existing customers and customers' complaints were dealt with in an antagonistic and unprofessional manner. The pursuer claimed that the breaches were such as to materially damage the goodwill in the brand that it had acquired, and the Court found (at [128]) that the vendors were in breach of contract "both in relation to the quality of the product manufactured and in relation to the treatment of customers who complained". The Court found that the incidence of customer claims increased dramatically in respect of product produced during the five month period.

The pursuer claimed that the damages flowing from these breaches resulted in ([134]) a significant loss of sales, and a consequential loss of profit on those sales. The Court found ([155] and [176]) that losses of sales of the branded product were caused by the breaches. The Court accepted that the evidence established a loss in sales ([227]).

The expert evidence assessed the revenues that were generated from the acquired assets and the revenues that would have been generated from the customer base but for the breach. This was assessed on the basis of a consideration of the actual and likely purchases made by all the vendor's customers acquired by the pursuer, making adjustments for individual customers whose decline in purchases could be attributed to specific individual reasons ([191], [229]–[230]). The assessment of the likely sales was made on the basis of various alternative methods and the results were then averaged out ([265]). The Court found that the evidence provided a reasonable estimate of the lost sales ([282]) and awarded damages to the pursuer as compensation for damage to their goodwill.

(v)   *Physical Injury to the Buyer or his Property*

Physical injury to the buyer, his family or his property

17–072   [*Add at the end of fn.561*]
In *Hi-Lite Electrical Ltd v Wolseley UK Ltd* [2011] EWHC 2153 (TCC), it was found that a fire causing damage to the claimant's business premises (hair salon) had not been caused by a defect in the goods supplied by the seller (an electrical pump) but by the acts of staff cutting a cable whilst cleaning away "gunk and hair" accumulated over the cable. The Judge went on to consider what the position would have been if he had found that the fire had been caused by a defect in the goods supplied. It had been submitted by the seller that the type of damage was too remote because it could not ordinarily be expected that an electrical fault in a submersible pump would lead to a fire. The Trial Judge said (at [215]) that he thought that the correct question was whether at the time of the contract a fire was not unlikely to result from a manufacturing defect in the pump. He thought that there was a clear logical sequence of events from the breach to the fire which satisfied the remoteness test of not unlikely to result—a defect in an electrical cable causing wires to break, causing arcing, sparks and heating causing the cable to ignite.

5.   REPAYMENT OF THE PRICE OR ADVANCE PAYMENTS

Restitution: recovery of money paid to the seller

17–090   [*Amend fn.711*]
Goff and Jones, *The Law of Unjust Enrichment* (8th edn, 2011), paras 12.10 *et seq*.

[*Add at the end of fn.717*]
For a thorough examination of the authorities on the recovery of monies paid where the consideration for the payment has failed, see *Giedo van der Garde BV v Force India Formula One Team* [2010] EWHC 2373 (QB) at [233]–[367]. In that case the plaintiff claimed recovery of USD 3 million which had been paid to the defendants in consideration of a racing car driver being permitted to test and practice a formula 1 racing car for a minimum of 6,000 km. The defendants repudiated the agreement after permitting the plaintiff to drive 2,004 km. Held after considering *Fibrosa Spolka Akcyjna v Fairbairn Lawson Combe Barbour* [1943] AC 32 and a large number of other authorities including *Ebrahim Dawood Ltd v Heath* (Est. 1927) [1961] 2 Lloyd's Rep. 512; *Biggerstaff v Rowatt's Wharf* [1896] 2 Ch. 93, *Ferguson v Sohl* (1992) 62 B.L.R. 95; *Rowland v Divall* [1923] 2 K.B. 500; *Goss v Chilcott* [1996] A.C. 788; *StoczniaGdanskc v Latvian Shipping Co* [1998] 1 W.L.R. 574; *Hunt v Silk* (1804) 5 East 449; *Warman v Southern Counties*

Car Finance Company [1949] 2 K.B. 577; *David Securities Pty Ltd v Commonwealth Bank of Australia* (1992) 175 C.L.R. 353 (High Court of Australia); *Whincup* v *Hughes* (1871) L.R. 6 C.P. 78; *Rover International Ltd v Cannon Film Sales Ltd* [1989] 1 WLR 912; *Barber v NSW Bank Plc* [1996] 1 W.L.R. 641; *Baltic Shipping Co* v *Dillon* (1992) 176 C.L.R. 344 (High Court of Australia); that the claim must fail on the ground that there had not been a total failure of consideration: "I am bound to say that I reach this conclusion with considerable regret, joining as I do the growing list of judges and academic writers who have expressed the view that the requirement of proof of total failure of consideration as a necessary condition for an award of restitution is unsatisfactory and liable in certain circumstances to work injustice."

6.   REMEDIES OTHER THAN CLAIMS TO MONEY

(d)   *Specific Performance for Delivery of the Goods*

"Specific or ascertained goods"

[*Insert at the beginning of fn.758*]   **17–097**
    Section 52 of the Sale of Goods Act 1979 was considered in *Astrazeneca UK Limited v Albemarle International Corporation* [2011] EWHC 1574 (Comm) at [303]–[305]. As the goods in question were neither specific nor ascertained the section was held inapplicable. The goods were pharmaceutical goods none of which were identified and agreed upon at the time the relevant order was placed. Nor were they ascertained goods. The Judge said (following Atkin L.J. in *Re Wait* [1927] 1 Ch. 606) that ascertained probably means identified in accordance with the agreement after the time the contract is made. Applying that definition he thought that the goods did not become ascertained until at the earliest they were shipped.

The types of goods for which the remedy is appropriate

[*Add at the end of fn.785*]   **17–099**
    In *SSL International Plc Ltd v TTK LIG Ltd* [2011] EWCA Civ 1170, at [87]–[95] no order was made under s.52 because the goods were neither specific nor ascertained (the claimants could not identify which goods related to which contract) and the Court was being asked to make an order that would require an unacceptable degree of supervision in a foreign land.

(g)   *Proprietary Claims to Possession or Damages*

Wrongful resale or retaking by the seller

[*Amend fn.850*]   **17–106**
Clerk and Lindsell on Torts (20th edn), para.17–114.

Part Seven

OVERSEAS SALES

CHAPTER 18

OVERSEAS SALES IN GENERAL

Note: The text of Chapters 18–21 of the Main Work contains many references to the 2nd edition of *Carver on Bills of Lading* (2005), which has been superseded by the 3rd edition (2011). So far as it relates to these Chapters, this Supplement would become hopelessly cluttered if all these references were updated in it; the necessary updating will be undertaken in the next edition of the Main Work. For the same reason, references to the 12th edition of Treitel on *The Law of Contract* by Peel (2007), which has been superseded by the 13th edition (2011), have not been updated in the parts of this Supplement which relate to Chapters 18–21 of the Main Work.

1. PRELIMINARY

INCOTERMS

18–002   [*Add at the end of fn.4*]
    See also *KG Bominflot Bunkergesellschaft für Mineraloele mbH & Co v Petroplus Marketing AG (The Mercini Lady)* [2010] EWCA Civ 1145; [2011] 1 Lloyd's Rep. 442, where an f.o.b. contract expressly incorporated INCOTERMS 2000, but nothing seems to have turned on this point.

2. DOCUMENTS OF TITLE TO GOODS

(a) *Bills of Lading*

(i) *Types of Bills of Lading*

Straight (or "non-negotiable") bills and sea waybills

18–024   [*Line 3, add new fn.152A after "transferability"*]

[152A] *e.g. AP Moeller Maersk A/S (trading as Maersk Line) v Sonaec Villas Cen Sad Fadoul* [2010] EWHC 355 (Comm); [2010] 2 All E.R. (Comm) 1159, where the court at [42] accepted the argument that a bill which provided for delivery "to a named consignee and was not made out to order" (at [37]) was a "straight" bill.

(ii) Bill of Lading as a Receipt

Effects of false statement as to shipment or receipt between shipper and carrier

[*fn.368, after "557" in line 1, add*] **18–049**
; and see *Newport City Council v Charles* [2008] EWCA Civ 1541; [2009] 1 W.L.R. 1884 at [27], viewing this position with "unease" (at [28]).

Bill signed by carrier personally

[*Add at the end of fn.417*] **18–056**
For the concept of an act (in this case, a signature) done by the company itself, see also the discussion of Companies Act 2006, s.44 in *Williams v Redcard Ltd* [2011] EWCA Civ 466; [2011] 4 All E.R. 444.

(iii) Bill of Lading as a Contractual Document

Bill of Lading as evidence of contract of carriage

[*Add at the end of fn.554*] **18–072**
For similar reasoning, see *PT Berlian Laju Tanker TBK v Nuse Shipping Ltd (The Aktor)* [2008] EWHC 1330 (Comm); [2008] 2 Lloyd's Rep. 246, where a recap email amounting to a "concluded contract for the sale of a ship" was "superseded by the final signed contract" in the form of a memorandum of agreement (at [60]).

Bill of Lading as a contract of carriage

[*Add at the end of fn.562*] **18–073**
; *cf. National Navigation Co v Endesa Generacion SA (The Wadi Sudr)* [2009] EWHC 196 (Comm); [2009] 1 Lloyd's Rep. 666 at [66] ("the contract contained in the bill of lading"). The defendant, to whom the bill was presumably transferred, was named in it as consignee. The decision was reversed on other grounds [2009] EWCA Civ 1397; [2010] 1 Lloyd's Rep. 193.

Terms of the bill of lading contract

[*fn.569, line 3, after "559;" add*] **18–074**
contrast *The Dolphina* [2011] SGHC 273; [2012] 1 Lloyd's Rep. 304 at [121]–[132] (discussing English authorities), where the words of the bill of lading were held to be sufficiently clear to incorporate a charterparty choice of (English) law clause.

[Add at the end of fn.569]

The requirements of the "more restrictive approach" referred to in fn.569 of Main Work, para.18–074 were held by Beatson J. to have been satisfied in *TTMI SARL v Statoil ASA* [2011] EWHC 1150 (Comm); [2011] 2 Lloyd's Rep. 220 at [51], where the issue was whether the parties (to the litigation) had "incorporated the terms of a contract between two other parties".

(iv) *Bill of Lading as a Document of Title*

Shipped bill made out to bearer or order

18–089 *[Add at the end of fn.671]*

See also *The Dolphina* [2011] SGHC 273; [2012] 1 Lloyd's Rep. 304 at [146]–[152], where the carrier's delivery of the goods without presentation of the (blank indorsed) bill of lading was held to be a breach of the contract of carriage, but the claimant had, for the reason stated in para.18–144 of this Supplement, no title to sue.

[Add at the end of fn.677]

See also *Carewins Development (China) Ltd v Bright Fortune Shipping Ltd* [2009] 1 HKLRD 409, discussing English authorities on fundamental breach and holding that the exemption clause in that case was not sufficiently clear to cover a carrier's breach in delivering goods shipped under a straight bill without presentation of the bill. For the requirement of production in the case of a straight bill, see Main Work, paras 18–095 to 18–098.

[Add at the end of fn.679]

Reasoning similar to that of *The Laemthong Glory* [2005] EWCA Civ 519; [2005] 1 Lloyd's Rep. 688 accounts for the outcome in *Far East Chartering Ltd v Binani Cement Ltd (The Jag Ravi)* [2012] EWCA Civ 180, affirming [2011] EWHC 1372 (Comm); [2011] 2 Lloyd's Rep. 309, where the LOI was addressed by the prospective receivers of the goods (A) to "The Owners/Disponent Owners/Charterers" of the carrying ship. The LOI was held at [42] to be "capable of acceptance by the charterers" (B) and to have given rise to a contract between A and B; and it was further held that C, the owners of the carrying ship, who had made the goods available to A without production of the bill of lading and had so incurred a liability covered by the LOI, could enforce the LOI against A by virtue of the Contract (Rights of Third Parties) Act 1999 (see at [36]). The judgment does not make it clear either exactly how the offer contained in the LOI had been accepted by B (as opposed to being "capable of acceptance" by them); or why that offer had not been accepted by C when they did the acts (referred to above) which had given rise to their liability. The point stressed here is that C's right of enforcement under the 1999 Act can only have arisen on the assumption that C were *not* parties to the LOI contract between A and B, since s.1(1) of that Act confers rights only on a person who "is *not* a party" to the contract in question (italics supplied).

18–096 *[Add at the end of fn.784]*

So far as *The Brij* [2001] 1 Lloyd's Rep. 431 (Hong Kong High Court) decides that a straight bill does not have be produced by the named consignee on claiming delivery of the goods, the case was overruled by *Carewins Development (China)*

Ltd v Bright Fortune Shipping Ltd [2009] 1 HKLRD 429 at [37] (Hong Kong Court of Final Appeal). The judgments in the *Carewins* case arguably support two views as to the legal basis of the requirements of production of a straight bill. One is that the requirement follows (as in the case of an order bill (Main Work, para.18–089)) from the nature of a straight bill (at [28]); the other is that the requirement follows from the terms of the document (at [29]; *cf.* Main Work, para.18–097). For further discussion of the *Carewins* case on the present point, see *Carver on Bills of Lading* (3rd edn, 2011), para.6–020.

[*Page 1221, line 9 at* "of the bill", *insert new fn.800A*]   **18–097**

800A In *Beluga Shipping GmbH & Co v Headway Shipping Ltd* [2008] F.C.A. 1791 the Federal Court of Australia held that bills of lading which were described (at [3]) as "non-negotiable" and therefore "straight", had to be produced to the carrier by the person claiming delivery. It was also said (at [13]) that "the bills require production of an original bill to obtain delivery of the cargo." Although the point is not entirely clear from the report (which does not give the text of the bills), this statement seems to mean that there was an express provision in the bill imposing the requirement of production. The case is therefore, to this extent at least, consistent with the view put forward in the text in the Main Work of this paragraph.

[*Add at the end of para.18–097*]
The view that the consignee named in a straight bill of lading is entitled, as against the carrier, to delivery of the goods only on production, presentation or surrender of bill to the carrier is further supported by the Hong Kong case of *Carewins Development (China) Ltd v Bright Fortune Shipping Ltd.*812A In that case, a carrier who delivered goods shipped under such a bill without production of it to an agent of the consignee named in it was accordingly held liable for breach of the contract of carriage.812B In support of this conclusion, the court relied, first, on authorities which had established the requirement of production of the bill where the bill was an order bill.812C But if, as is argued in para.18–101 of the Main Work, the requirement of production was in these cases the *consequence*, and not the cause of the "negotiability" of such a bill, then the argument that the requirement extends to bills which are *not* "negotiable" is, at least on historical grounds, open to question. Secondly, the requirement of production was said to be based on considerations of commercial convenience. One such consideration was that the requirement protects the interests of the shipper as it enables him, by withholding the bill, to ensure that he will be paid for the goods.812D But if this is the reason for the requirements, then it is hard to see why it does not extend to the case where the carriage document is a sea waybill; and the judgment recognises that in such a case there is *no* need for the carriage document to be produced to the carrier.812E Another such reason for the requirement is said to be that it relieves the master of the carrying ship from the need (in cases of doubt812F) "to resolve ambiguities as to whether a document is a straight bill or an order bill".812G This may be true, but once again the same kind of difficulty could arise in one of the borderline cases (discussed in para.18–025 of the Main Work) in which it is not clear whether the carriage document is a bill of lading or a sea waybill. Such difficulties would be mitigated, if not entirely eliminated, if it were made clear what exactly was the legal basis for the requirement of production in the case of a straight bill. The

judgments in the *Carewins* case[812H] arguably support two answers to this question. One is that the requirement of production follows from "the nature of the contract between shipper and carrier contained in the bill of lading"[812I]; on this view the requirement of production applies to straight bills in general,[812J] in the same way as it applies to order bills.[812K] The second view is that the requirement follows from "the terms of the bill of lading".[812L] Thus in the *Carewins* case it was said to follow from the provision usually found in bill of lading attestation clauses that, where bills are (as in that case they were) issued in a set of several original parts, "one . . . being accomplished the others to stand void"[812M]: on this view, the requirement is based on an implied term,[812N] or on the construction,[812O] of the bill of lading.

The distinction between the two views here discussed is not a mere matter of semantics. It would assume practical importance where there was nothing in the document that bore, one way or the other, on the question of implication or construction; and also if the force of law were given to the Rotterdam Rules.[812P] The effect of the Rules on the point here under consideration is discussed in para.18–035 of the Main Work. Under those Rules, a straight bill of lading would be a "non-negotiable" transport document[812Q]; and the Rules also distinguish between a non-negotiable instrument *simpliciter* and one "that indicates that it shall be surrendered in order to obtain delivery of the goods".[812R] This distinction would make no sense in relation to documents now known as straight bills if the requirement of surrender applied to all such documents; and so the distinction supports the view that the requirement stems, not (as in the case of order bills) from the inherent nature of the document,[812S] but rather from express or implied terms in it which "indicate" that such a requirement must be satisfied.

[812A] [2009] 1 HKLRD 429 (Hong Kong Court of Final Appeal), overruling at [37], so far as *contra*, *The Brij* [2001] 1 Lloyd's Rep. 431 (Hong Kong High Court).

[812B] The shipper had sold the goods to the consignee named in the bill but had not been paid for them.

[812C] *Carewins* case, above fn.812A at [21]–[23].

[812D] *ibid.*, at [27].

[812E] *ibid.*, at [30].

[812F] See Main Work, para.18–097, after fn.806.

[812G] *Carewins* case, above fn.812A, at [85].

[812H] Above, fn.812A.

[812I] At [2].

[812J] *i.e.* unless the terms of the bill expressly or by implication dispense with the requirement of production.

[812K] *Carewins* case, above fn.812A, at [28]. For the requirement of production in the case of order bills, see Main Work para.18–089.

[812L] *Carewins* case, above fn.812A, at [29].

[812M] At [33]; *cf.* Main Work, para.18–097 at fn.806.

[812N] At [2], [85]; *cf.* Main Work, para.18–097 at fn.806.

[812O] See *Attorney General of Belize v Belize Telecom Ltd* [2009] UKPC 10; [2009] 1 W.L.R. 1988.

[812P] Main Work, para.18–011.

[812Q] Article 1(17), Main Work, para.18–135.

[812R] See Main Work, para.18–035 fn.1125.

812S Article 47(2) of the Rules envisages the possibility that a "negotiable transport document" (Main Work, para.18–126) may expressly dispense with the requirement of surrender. An order bill would be such a document (see Main Work, para.18–089 at fn.691); but if, unusually, it expressly dispensed with the requirements of production, it could not be a document of title at common law: see Main Work, para.18–133 at fnn.1115–1116.

Document of title function?

[Add at the end of fn.839]   **18–100**

References in *Beluga Shipping GmbH & Co v Headway Shipping Ltd* [2008] F.C.A.1791 to the bills in that case as "documents of title" are explicable on the ground that they are such documents in the second of the two common law senses discussed in paras 18–007 and 18–008 of the Main Work, *i.e.* in the sense of documents which have to be produced to the carrier by the person claiming delivery of the goods: see this Supplement para.18–097 fn.800A. No issue arose in that case as to the "conveyancing" function of the bills, the only dispute being between the parties to the contract of carriage. If the statement that "the arrangement between [two of these parties] appeared to require the issue of non-negotiable . . . bills of lading" means that the bills were required to be *marked* "non-negotiable", then they clearly were not "documents of title" in the common law sense described in Main Work, para.18–007: see Main Work, para.18–102. Even if they were not so marked, it is submitted that they were not, in the absence of proof of custom of the kind described in Main Work, para.18–007, documents of this kind: see Main Work, para.18–101.

[Add at the end of para.18–100]

In *Carewins Development (China) Ltd v Bright Fortune Shipping Ltd*859A the straight bill there under discussion was repeatedly described as a "document of title", but was also said not to be "negotiable".859B It follows from these statements that the bill was a "document of title" only in the sense described in para.18–008 of the Main Work, that is in the sense of a document that must be produced to the carrier by the person claiming delivery of the goods. It must be repeated that the use of the expression "document of title" to refer to a document merely on account of its having this characteristic is of relatively recent origin.859C The bill was *not* a document of title in the older, traditional sense of "document of title" discussed in para.18–007 of the Main Work, that is, of a document, the transfer of which could perform the "conveyancing function" described in para.18–088 of the Main Work. As one of the judgments in the *Carewins* case puts the point, the straight bills there under consideration were "not negotiable in the sense of being freely transferable to subsequent holders by indorsement and delivery".859D The force of the further statement that "there is no valid reason why the essential characteristic of a bill of lading as a document of title should depend on whether it is negotiable"859E must, with respect, depend on what is that "essential characteristic". If, as is argued in para.18–101 of the Main Work, the requirement of production of an order bill of lading is the consequence and not the cause of its being "negotiable", then it would seem that its "essential" characteristic *is* its "negotiability" and it was accepted in the *Carewins* case that the bills there did not have this characteristic; nor did that case raise any issue as to what we have called the "conveyancing function"[859F] of order bills. Finally, if (as seems to be not uncommon) a straight bill expressly provided that it was "not negotiable" or "non-negotiable", then it would follow from the reasoning of para.18–102 of the Main Work that the bill could not be a document of title in the traditional common law sense described in para.18–007 of the Main Work, and (to put the same point in another way) that it could not be used to perform what we have called the "conveyancing function" of such a document.

[859A] [2009] 1 HKLRD 429 (Hong Kong Court of Final Appeal); para.18–097 of this Supplement.
[859B] [2009] 1 HKLRD 429 at [9], [19], [40], [76].
[859C] See Main Work, para.18–008.
[859D] *Carewins* case, above fn.859A, at [9]; for the meaning of "negotiable" in this context, see Main Work, para.18–111. It can be inferred from the statement here quoted that no custom such as that described in Main Work, para.18–007 was proved in relation to the bills.
[859E] *Carewins* case, above fn.859A, at [27].
[859F] Main Work, para.18–088. Nor did any such issue arise in *The Rafaela S* [2009] UKHL 11; [2005] A.C. 423 (Main Work, para.18–097), on dicta in which much reliance was placed in the *Carewins* case, above fn.859A.

"Transferability"

18–104   [*fn.890, line 4, after* "generally'" *add*]
; *Carewins Development (China) Ltd v Bright Fortune Shipping Ltd* [2009] 1 HKLRD 409 at [40].

More than one set of bills of lading

18–122   [*fn.1041, line 10 after* "18–088)." *add*]
The Brij [2001] 1 Lloyd's Rep. 431 was overruled on the point discussed in para.18–096 fn.784 of this Supplement in *Carewins Development (China) Ltd v Bright Fortune Shipping Ltd* [2009] 1 HKLRD 429 (Hong Kong Court of Final Appeal). For the *Carewins* case, see this Supplement para.18–097.

(vi)   *Acquisition of Contractual Rights*

Lawful holder

18–144   [*line 13, delete* "delivery." *and insert*]
delivery[1194]; and it has been held in Singapore that "any endorsement" meant "any *valid* endorsement", so that no rights of suit were acquired by a person to whom the bill had been delivered after having been fraudulently indorsed in blank.[1194A]

[1194a] *The Dolphina* [2011] SGHC 273; [2012] 1 Lloyd's Rep. 304 at [166], [178], [179]; the bill of lading in question was held to have been governed by English law by virtue of an effective provision in the bill incorporating a

charterparty provision to this effect: see *ibid.,* at [121]–[131]; and this Supplement para.18–074. Hence, transfer of rights under the bill was governed by the Carriage of Goods by Sea Act 1992. The person to whom the bill had been delivered was, however, held to have a good claim in tort for conspiracy: see at [282].

Spent bill of lading

[Add at the end of fn.1240]   **18–153**
A bill of lading is not "spent" by delivery of the goods to a person to whom the bill of lading has been delivered after having been indorsed, if the indorsement was ineffective, *e.g.* because it was vitiated by fraud: see *The Dolphina* [2011] SGHC 273; [2012] 1 Lloyd's Rep. 304 at [160]–[164]. Hence, although the bill of lading in that case was governed by English law (see this Supplement para.18–144) there was no discussion in the judgment of Carriage of Goods by Sea Act 1992, s.2(2).

Rights of original shipper

[Add at the end of fn.1261]   **18–154**
In *Landfast (Anglia) Ltd v Cameron Taylor One Ltd* [2008] EWHC 343 (TCC); 117 Con. L.R. 533 at [29] it was said that if, as a result of A's breach of A's contract with B, C (an assignee of B's rights under that contract) had suffered loss, then it would be arguable that C could sue A in respect of that loss even though no loss had (as a result of the breach) been suffered by B.

[Add at the end of fn.1272]
Cf. *Marquess of Aberdeen and Temair v Turcan Connell* [2008] CSOH 183; [2009] SCLR 336 at [45].

Original shipper's rights independent of contract

[Add at the end of fn.1289]   **18–155**
For a bailee's non-contractual duty, see also *Yearworth v Bristol NHS Trust* [2009] EWCA Civ 37; [2010] 1 Q.B. 1, where such liability was said at [48] to be *sui generis, i.e.* to arise neither in contract or in tort; for this case, see also this Supplement, para.18–155 fn.1307C.

[After "as such." *in the third line after fn.1307, add]*
The reference,[1307A] in other words, is to terms of the contract of carriage which *restrict* the shipper's rights. It does not seem that the concept of bailment on terms could have *extended* those rights, *i.e.* entitled a shipper who had lost his rights under the contract of carriage to claim the benefits of positive duties going beyond the custodial duties normally imposed on a bailee at common law and alleged to have arisen from a "particular"[1307B] or "specific"[1307C] promise made by the carrier.

[1307A] In the passage cited in the Main Work on p.1280 at fnn.1304–1306.
[1307B] *Yearworth v North Bristol NHS Trust* [2009] EWCA Civ 37; [2010] Q.B. 1 at [48]
[1307C] *ibid.*, at [58], distinguishing between a duty alleged to have arisen from such a promise and "the duty owed by every gratuitous bailee". It is the latter duty

which is referred to, in the text above, as the custodial duty "normally imposed on a bailee at common law". As the *Yearworth* case itself shows, the distinction between the two types of duty can give rise to difficulties since they are not mutually exclusive; and since the second of the above categories may be too general: for example, the scope of the duty "owed by every . . . bailee" may depend on a "specific promise"—*e.g.* as to where goods are to be stored, or whether they are to be refrigerated or heated during carriage.

Extent of rights exercisable

18–161　　*[Add at the end of fn.1385]*

The cause of action remains, nevertheless, A's "*own* cause of action" (*Pace Shipping Co Ltd v Churchgate Nigeria Ltd (The Pace) (No.2)* [2010] EWHC 2828 (Comm); [2011] 1 Lloyd's Rep. 537 at [28], [30]. Hence if A's action was begun before, but s.2(4) was first invoked after, the period of limitation in respect of it had expired, then A's claim will not be time-barred.

(vii)　*Imposition of Contractual Liabilities*

Making a claim under the contract of carriage

18–169　　*[Add at the end of fn.1443]*

For an application of the policy against making banks liable on bills of lading merely by reason of their having a security interest in the goods, see *Fortis Bank SA/NV v Indian Overseas Bank (No.2)* [2011] EWHC 538; [2012] 1 All E.R. 41 at [67]. It was there accepted (at [59]) that s.3 of the Carriage of Goods by Sea Act "did not apply to this case" as the bank had neither taken nor demanded delivery of the goods, nor made any claim under the contract of carriage. But the policy referred to in the text above was invoked to rebut the argument that the bank was liable on the bill at common law, *i.e.* on the ground that the shipper had acted as the bank's agent by virtue of having taken out bills of lading in which the bank was named as consignee: see below, para.19–092 fn.632.

(x)　*Liability in Tort*

Buyer having no proprietary interest in the goods

18–189　　*[Add at the end of fn.1582]*

In *Shell UK Ltd v Total UK Ltd* [2010] EWCA Civ 180; [2010] 3 All E.R. 793 it was held that a claim for economic loss resulting from damage to property could be brought by a beneficial owner so long as he joined the legal owner of the property as a party to the proceedings. It was said at [131] and [144] that *The Aliakmon* [1986] A.C. 785 (Main Work, para.18–089 at fn.1578) had not concluded the question of the availability of such a remedy to an equitable owner. It seems, on the contrary, that the possibility of such a person's having a claim in tort was foreshadowed by Lord Brandon's statement at p.812 in *The Aliakmon* that, if the claimant were "the equitable owner of the goods and no more, then he must join the legal owner as a party to the action". In *The Aliakmon* the question did not directly arise as the buyer did *not* have had any equitable title to the goods (at p.812).

[Add at the end of fn.1590]
Cf. Robinson v PE Jones (Contractors) Ltd [2011] EWCA Civ 9; [2011] B.L.R. 206, a building contract case, in which it was held that the builder's liability to his client (the other party to the contract) for economic loss caused by defects in the work arose in contract only, and not in tort, as there was no "assumption of responsibility" by the builder to the client which could give rise to "duties of care co-extensive with their [*i.e.* the builder's] contractual duties" (at [68], [72], [83], [84]).

[fn.1592, line 12 after "personal injury." add]
For another case applying the "exclusivity principle" of the air carriage convention in cases of personal injury, see *Hook v British Airways Plc* [2011] EWHC 379 (QB); [2011] 1 All E.R. (Comm) 1128 at [29], [35].

Concurrent liability in contract and tort

[Add at the end of fn.1630]   **18–191**
For further recent cases restricting concurrent liability in tort between parties in a contractual relationship with one another, see *Whitecap Leisure Ltd v John H Rundle Ltd* [2008] EWCA Civ 429; [2008] 2 Lloyd's Rep. 216 and *Robinson v PE Jones (Contractors) Ltd* [2011] EWCA Civ 9; [2011] B.L.R. 206 (this Supplement, para.18–189 fn.1590). Neither of these cases arose in the context of contracts for the carriage by sea, but their reasoning on the issue of concurrent liability in contract and tort could be applied in such a context.

(b) Sea Waybills

(i) Transfer of Contractual Rights

Rights of original shipper

[line 7, add new fn.1657A after "it was made."]   **18–200**

1657A See *AP Moeller-Maersk A/S (trading as Maersk Line) v Sonaec Villas Cen Sad Fadoul* [2010] EWHC 355 (Comm); [2010] 2 All E.R. (Comm) 1159 at [37], stating that A's rights of suit were "transferred to the named consignee [C] as soon as the bill was signed." Although a contract of carriage may be "made" before the bill is signed (Main Work, para.18–072), the "contract of carriage" with which we are here concerned, is the contract defined as such by Carriage of Goods by Sea Act 1992, s.5(1), *viz.*, the "contract contained in or evidenced by that . . . sea way bill."

[Add new para.18–200A]

The *Maersk Line* case

The view that, where the contract of carriage is contained in or evidenced by a   **18–200A**
sea waybill, the original shipper's right to redirect the goods survives the acquisition of rights[1659A] under that contract by the consignee named in the bill is supported by the *Maersk Line* case,[1659B] where goods had been sold on f.o.b. terms and were shipped under a bill of lading which had not been made out to

order and hence was "for the purposes of the 1992 Act . . . to be treated as a sea waybill".[1659C] The bill did not make it clear whether it was the seller or the buyer who was the shipper,[1659D] but the agent to whom the bill had been given had, in pursuance of an order made in Chinese proceedings, "given up",[1659E] the bill to the seller "on the footing that [the seller] was the shipper [of the goods] and entitled to the . . . bill".[1959F] It followed that the seller "became the party entitled to the rights of the shipper under the bill, even if it had not done so before"; that "those rights included a right to order the goods to be delivered otherwise than to the named consignee"[1659G]; and that this right had not been lost merely because that consignee had acquired rights of suit under the contract of carriage by virtue of s.2 (1)(b) of the Carriage of Goods by Sea Act 1992. It should be emphasised that the seller's right to redirect had not vested in him as the result of the operation of the 1992 Act. That Act governs the *transfer* of rights, usually (in the case of goods carried under a sea waybill) from a shipper to a named consignee. The seller's right to redirect had vested in him as a matter of common law from the time of the issue of the bill; and this is true even though he may not have been judicially identified as shipper until some later time. It is only in this sense that he at this latter time "became" the party in whom that right was vested.[1659H] The only relevance to this point of the 1992 Act was that the seller was not deprived of his common law right to redirect when rights of suit under the waybill had been transferred to and vested in the buyer by virtue of s.2(1)(b) of the Act. The seller's right to redirect survived this transfer and continued, by virtue of s.2(5) of the 1992 Act,[1659I] to be vested in the seller as an original party to the contract of carriage. In the exercise of this right, the seller (not having been paid under the contract of sale) surrendered the bill to the carrier[1659J] who, at the seller's request issued a second bill making the goods deliverable to the order of the seller[1659K]; and these steps amounted to the termination of the original contract of carriage and its substitution by "a new contract of carriage (by way of a new bill of lading)",[1659L] so that the first bill became "inoperative".[1659M] The buyer still not having paid the price to the seller, the latter resold the goods to a second buyer (B2) and surrendered the second bill to the carrier, who issued a third bill of lading identifying B2 as the consignee and delivered the goods to B2 in accordance with the terms of the third bill. One of the issues that arose was whether the original buyer had title to sue the carrier under the first bill; and a negative answer was given to this question since as a result of the steps taken by the seller (and described above) "the first bill was cancelled and replaced with the second and later the third bill of lading".[1659N]

[1659A] By virtue of Carriage of Goods by Sea Act 1992, s.2(1)(b); Main Work, para.18–193.

[1659B] *AP Moller-Maersk A/S (trading as Maersk Line) v Sonaec Villas Cen Sad Fadoul* [2010] EWHC 355 (Comm); [2010] 2 All E.R. (Comm) 1159 (the *Maersk Line* case; see also this Supplement, para.20–073A.

[1659C] *Maersk Line* case, above fn.1659A at [28]; Main Work, para.18–192.

[1659D] The shippers named in the bill were B and D Co Ltd "p/c (*pour compte de*) Vernal [a subsidiary or associate of the buyer] and Yekalon [the seller]". The meaning of "*pour compte de*" was "not entirely clear" (at [43]). A "possible view" was that B and D was "contracting for the carriage on behalf of [the buyer]" but also for "the seller" (at [44]); though this view gives rise to the difficulty that the interests of these parties were "potentially antithetical" (at [43]).

[1659E] *Maersk Line* case, above fn.1659A, at [13].

[1659F] *ibid.,* at [52].

[1659G] *ibid.*

[1659H] As the words "even if . . . before" (quoted at fn.1659G above from [52] of the *Maersk Line* case) indicate.

[1659I] See the "tailpiece" to s.2(5), quoted in Main Work, para.18–200 after fn.1658.

[1659J] *Maersk Line* case, above fn.1659A, at [14].

[1659K] *ibid.*

[1659L] *ibid.,* at [39].

[1659M] *ibid.,* at [29].

[1659N] *ibid.,* at [54].

3.   PASSING OF PROPERTY

In general

[*fn.1991, line 6, after* "at [6];" *add*]   **18–251**
See also cl.15 of the f.o.b. contract in *KG Bominflot Bunkergesellschaft für Mineraloele mbH & Co v Petroplus Marketing AG (The Mercini Lady)* [2010] EWCA Civ 1145; [2011] 1 Lloyd's Rep. 442 at [28].

4.   LOSS OR DETERIORATION IN TRANSIT

(a)   *Commercial Sales*

Implied undertaking that goods can endure normal transit

[*Add at the end of fn.2219*]   **18–297**
In *KG Bominflot Bunkergesellschaft für Mineraloele mbH & Co v Petroplus Marketing AG (The Mercini Lady)* [2010] EWCA Civ 1145; [2011] 1 Lloyd's Rep. 442 the Court of Appeal, for reasons discussed in para.18–298A of this Supplement, held that buyers of gasoil which was admitted to be in conformity with the contract when shipped, were not entitled to reject the goods on the ground that they were not of the contractual specification at a destination port, reversing the decision at first instance that there was an implied condition at common law that the goods should "remain on specification for a reasonable time after delivery" (see at [23]). Rix L.J. said at [44] that this "additional implied term was simply not part of the intention of the parties to this contract and would not have been understood by reasonable merchants to have been part of its meaning" (see *Attorney General of Belize v Belize Telecom Ltd* [2009] UKPC 10, [2009] 1 W.L.R. 1988). This passage might suggest that, contrary to the submission in Main Work, para.18–297 fn.2219, the reasoning of the *Belize* case was also relevant to the existence and scope of implied undertaking discussed in that paragraph; but the

judgment makes no reference to the question whether that reasoning applies to established terms implied in law, which are often based on policy considerations as opposed to an investigation of the intention of the parties. That intention is relevant to such an implied term in the sense that it may negative the existence of the term in a particular case, especially where the alleged term is not an established, but a "novel" one, as in *The Mercini Lady*; and it is these factors that appear to account for the decision in that case.

[*Add at the end of fn.2222*]

KG Bominflot Bunkergesellschaft für Mineraloele mbH & Co v Petroplus Marketing AG (The Mercini Lady) [2010] EWCA Civ 1145; [2011] 1 Lloyd's Rep. 442 reverses the decision at first instance referred to in Main Work, para.18–297 fn.2222. But on the point for which the first instance decision is there cited, Rix L.J. said ([2010] EWCA Civ 1145 at [55]) that the "*Mash and Murrell* implication", though referred to by Lord Diplock as a "warranty", was "part of the meaning to be attached to what is now the section 14(2) implied condition." To this extent, he seems to agree with the statement quoted in Main Work, para.18–297 fn.2222, classifying this "implication" as a condition.

[*Add at the end of fn.2228*]

In *KG Bominflot Bunkergesellschaft für Mineraloele mbH & Co v Petroplus Marketing AG (The Mercini Lady)* [2010] EWCA Civ 1145; [2011] 1 Lloyd's Rep. 442, the decision at first instance (cited in Main Work, para.18–297 fnn.2222 and 2227) was reversed on grounds stated in para.18–298A of this Supplement. In the Court of Appeal, Rix L.J. at [16] referred with apparent approval to Main Work, para.18–297 fn.2228, thus perhaps sharing the scepticism there expressed about the suggestion made at first instance (see Main Work, para.18–297 at fn.2227) that the implied undertaking discussed in that paragraph could now be regarded as an application of Sale of Goods Act 1979, s.14(2). This inference, based on [16] of Rix L.J.'s judgment is, however, not easy to reconcile with the later passage from [55] of that judgment which is quoted in para.18–297 fn.2222 of this Supplement. The relationship between the common law implied undertaking (discussed in para.18–297 of the Main Work) and s.14(2) therefore awaits final determination. As is pointed out in Main Work, para.18–297 after fn.2228, the point is of more than merely theoretical interest.

[*Add new para.18–298A*]

The Mercini Lady

18–298A   The view that the implied undertaking formulated in the *Mash & Murrell*[2235A] case (and discussed in para.18–297 of the Main Work) commonly relates to the time of shipment derives further, if indirect, support from the decision of the Court of Appeal in *The Mercini Lady*.[2235B] In that case, gasoil was sold f.o.b. Antwerp; the contract provided for a maximum level of sediment; for quality to be determined by a mutually agreed inspector "basis shoretank", and for that determination to be final and binding on both parties (cl.12); for the buyer to assume "all risks" pertaining to the product when it passed the vessel's permanent hose connection (cl.15); and it excluded any "guarantees, warranties or misrepresentations . . . beyond the description of the oil set forth in this agreement" (cl.18). The gasoil was inspected at Antwerp where the inspector certified the sediment level to be below the maximum specified in (and so in accordance with) the contract. After a four-day voyage, the cargo was retested at the destination port and found to be "off-specification as to sediment."[2235C] The buyer rejected the goods and a number of preliminary issues fell to be determined by the Court of Appeal. The issue of particular interest in the context of the present discussion was whether a term was to be implied at common law to the effect that, even though the goods were "on specification" on delivery, they should remain in that condition for a reasonable time thereafter. At first instance, Field J. had held that such a term was to be implied, but this view was rejected by the Court of Appeal. Rix L.J. (with whom Maurice Kay and Patten L.JJ. agreed) said that, as it was admitted by the buyer that the gasoil was "within contractual specification on loading and delivery", it was "not easy to see" how the cargo could "nevertheless be delivered in breach of contract in a matter going to its specification . . . at any rate so long as that specification does not test durability".[2235D] He also distinguished between a "continuing warranty" (*i.e.* one which "would guarantee the condition of the goods after delivery") and a "prospective warranty" (*i.e.* one which "relates only to the time of delivery, but looks prospectively into the future and asks whether the goods, *as at the time of delivery*, were in the condition which the buyer was entitled to expect under the contract."[2235E] In *The Mercini Lady* the alleged common law implied term was "in effect to be used as a continuing warranty, even while the buyer eschews that ambition."[2235F] In this respect, that implication differed from the *Mash & Murrell* warranty[2235G]; and this no doubt accounts for the fact that the implication on which the buyer relied in *The Mercini Lady* was repeatedly described as a "novel" one.[2235H] The Court of Appeal held that there was "nothing to suggest, let alone require the alleged implication."[2235I] There was no support for it as a matter either of implication or interpretation. It was "simply not part of the intention of the parties to this contract"[2235J]; on the contrary, it was "clear that the specification has to be met at the time of delivery"[2235K]; this position was accepted by the buyer; and the provision that, after delivery, the buyer "assumes all risks" covered the "risk of transport" and that of "cargo instability."[2235L] It followed that the alleged common law term "which would put the seller in breach where goods of the contractual specification have been delivered but where there is subsequently (for an unspecified reason) a change cannot be implied *in this contract* even if the reason for that change were to be that the goods were not capable of maintaining their specification . . ."[2235M] A number of points arising from this decision call for comment in the present context.

First, counsel for the buyer did not, in the Court of Appeal, rely on the *Mash & Murrell* case[2235N] in support of the allegation that the seller was in breach by reason of the fact that the goods were off-specification at the port of destination. The most plausible reason why counsel did not so rely is to be found in the rule (discussed in para.18–298 of the Main Work) that the *Mash & Murrell* implication commonly relates to the condition of the goods at the time of shipment. In *The Mercini Lady* the goods had before that time been certified, in a way that bound both parties, as being within the specification; and the buyer admitted that "the gasoil *was* within the specification limits at the time of loading and delivery."[2235O] In the typical *Mash & Murrell* situation, the defect which leads to the deterioration of the goods must *exist* at that time, though it may then be latent and become apparent only at (or within a reasonable time of) the end of the transit. In such cases, the distinction between a defect which at the time of shipment is latent and one which comes into being at some later time may sometimes give rise to factual difficulties; but as a matter of principle the distinction is clear. In *The Mercini Lady* the buyer's admission referred to above[2235P] made it impossible for him to rely on the *Mash & Murrell* implication and led to his reliance on the "novel"[2235P] (and hence different) common law implied term discussed above.

Secondly, the judgment in *The Mercini Lady* differs from that in the *Mash & Murrell* case in that it does not contain any general statement about the possibility of implying the "novel" common law term (on which the buyer relied) into all f.o.b. contracts, let along into other types of overseas sales. Rix L.J.'s conclusion in *The Mercini Lady* is that the alleged term "cannot be implied *in this contract*"[2235Q]; and in reaching this conclusion he relies on a number of terms of the contract with which the alleged implication would be inconsistent. One such term was that which made it "clear that the specification has to be met at the time of delivery", that the quality inspector's certificate should be "conclusive" and "that specification should be determined conclusively at loading" or even before then (*i.e.* "basis shoretank")[2235R]; another was the term by which "[a]fter delivery" the buyer "assumes all risks", including the risks of "transport" and of "cargo instability".[2235S] The judgment, however, qualifies both these points: the first by the words "so long as that specification does not test durability"[2235T] and the second by the words "unless that risk has already been undertaken by the seller under a term of the contract which relates to the condition of the cargo pre-delivery."[2235U] The second of these qualifications may give rise to the difficulties that the certificate did relate to the condition of the gasoil "pre-delivery", *i.e.* while it was still in the shoretanks, while under an f.o.b. contract delivery would not normally occur until shipment,[2235V] and that before then the risk would, under the rule normally applicable to f.o.b. contracts *be* on the seller[2235W]; though it would be a matter for debate whether the "risk of cargo instability" had, in such a case "already been undertaken" by the seller under the contract, or had simply been imposed on him by law. The judgment does indeed, discuss the question whether such "inherent vice", if not intended to be covered by the certification clause, would amount to a breach of the implied term that the goods were of satisfactory quality[2235X]; but the reference here appears to be to the statutory implied term under s.14(2) of the Sale of Goods Act 1979, rather than to the "novel" common law term which is the subject of the present discussion.

A final group of problems concerns the relationship between the *Mash & Murrell* implied term as it was generally understood before *The Mercini Lady* and the reasoning of the latter case so far as it rejects the "novel" implication on which the buyer there relied. To the extent to which that reasoning is based on cl.15 of the contract (by which risk and title passed to the buyer when the gasoil passed the vessel's permanent hose connection) it gives rise to the difficulty that, so far as passing of risk is concerned, this clause merely states the general common law rule that under an f.o.b. contract risk passes on shipment.[2235Y] To this extent, therefore, it might seem that the reasoning could be used to undermine the *Mash & Murrell* implied term itself, whether or not the contract expressly provided for risk to pass on shipment since it would, in any event, pass at that point. But the

[86]

appearance is, it is submitted, deceptive, since the general rules as to risk may be displaced where the deterioration of the goods is due to the seller's breach of contract[2235Z]; and breach of the *Mash & Murrell* implied term is merely one illustration of this exception to the general rule relating to the passing of risk under f.o.b. contracts. This argument was not open to the buyer in *The Mercini Lady* by reason of the certification clause in the contract in that case, and of the buyer's admission that the gasoil was "within the contractual specification on loading and delivery."[2235AA] In a typical *Mash & Murrell* case, by contrast, the goods at that time are *not* (though they may appear to be) in conformity with the contract. A variant of the problem here under discussion arises where the seller is alleged to be in breach of a term relating to the "durability" of the goods. In *The Mercini Lady* Rix L.J. said that, once it was "admitted that the cargo *was* delivered *within* specification," it was "hard to see how later events can render its delivery as a breach of contract in a matter defined by that same specification (at any rate as long as that specification does not test durability) . . ."[2235AB] A term relating to durability of goods may be express[2235AC] or implied[2235AD]; and where a breach of such a term is alleged it is perhaps no more than a question of semantics whether the breach occurs at the time of delivery or at the later time when the lack of durability becomes apparent. On the former view, lack of "durability" could come within the *Mash & Murrell* implication as a matter of common law, even if the inability of commodities to endure normal transit did amount to a breach of the statutorily implied term under s.14(2) of the Sale of Goods Act 1979,[2235AE] so far as it relates to the characteristic of "durability." Conversely, it is arguable that, just as the certification clause in *The Mercini Lady* contract (followed by the issue of the certificate in that case) was one ground for the conclusion that the "novel" term could not be implied, so a clause in similar terms *could* negative the *Mash & Murrell* implied term in circumstances in which such an implication would *prima facie* have arisen; whether the term *would* have this effect would depend on the construction of the contract as a whole.[2235AF]

[2235A] *Mash & Murrell Ltd v Joseph I Emanuel Ltd* [1961] 1 W.L.R. 862 at p.865; Main Work para.18–297.

[2235B] *KG Bominflot Bunkergesellschaft für Mineraloele mbH & Co v Petroplus Marketing AG (The Mercini Lady)* [2010] EWCA Civ 1145; [2011] 1 Lloyd's Rep. 442.

[2235C] At [7].

[2235D] At [16].

[2235E] At [18], italics supplied.

[2235F] At [24].

[2235G] See at [21].

[2235H] At [1], [25], [39].

[2235I] At [39].

[2235J] At [44], referring to *Attorney General of Belize v Belize Telecom Ltd* [2009] UKPC 10, [2009] 1 W.L.R. 1988. As the words "in this contract" in the passage quoted above (and used also at [68]) indicate, the Court of Appeal in *The Mercini Lady* was concerned with the question whether the alleged "novel" (see above at fn.2235H) term was to be implied into a particular contract. In this respect, that term differed from the *Mash & Murrell* implied term which applies to a class (or classes) of contracts and was thus a term implied in law. For this reason, the argument that the reasoning of the *Belize* case does not affect the *Mash & Murrell* implication (see Main Work para.18–297 fn.2219) would not apply to the "novel" implication in *The Mercini Lady*.

[2235K] At [40].

[2235L] *ibid.*

[2235M] At [63], italics supplied.

[2235N] At [22]—"except incidentally": *i.e.* in relation to the point whether the words of cl.18 of the contract in *The Mercini Lady* were to be construed as excluding liability for breach of the alleged implied term.

[2235O] [2010] EWCA Civ 1145 at [40].

[2235P] At fn.2235O above.

[2235P] At [1], [25], [39].

[2235Q] At [63], italics supplied.

[2235R] At [40].

[2235S] At [40].

[2235T] At [16].

[2235U] At [40].

[2235V] See Main Work para.20–018.

[2235W] See Main Work para.20–094.

[2235X] [2010] EWCA Civ 1145 at [42].

[2235Y] See Main Work para.20–094. So far as "title" (*i.e.* property) is concerned, cl.15 *varies* the general common law rule as to the passing of property under f.o.b. contracts: see Main Work paras 20–082, 20–087.

[2235Z] See Main Work paras 18–298, 18–301.

[2235AA] At [40]; above fn.2235O.

[2235AB] [2010] EWCA Civ 1145 at [16].

[2235AC] *e.g. Shanklin Peer Ltd v Detel Products Ltd* [1951] 2 K.B. 854, where an express term as to durability had given rise to a collateral contract.

[2235AD] *e.g.* Sale of Goods Act 1979, s.14(2B)

[2235AE] See Main Work para.18–297.

[2235AF] See *Johnstone v Bloombury Health Authority* [1992] 1 Q.B. 333.

Applicability to f.o.b. contracts

18–299   [*Add at the end of the paragraph*]
The decision in *The Mercini Lady* has been reversed by the Court of Appeal,[2242A] where it became clear that the implied term on which the buyer relied differed from that based on the *Mash & Murrell* case[2242B] and discussed in paras 18–297 and 18–298 of the Main Work. It was therefore not necessary for the Court of Appeal to resolve the conflict of judicial opinion, discussed in para.18–299 of the Main Work, as to the scope of the *Mash & Murrell* implied term.[2242C]

[2242A] *K G Bominflot Bunkergesellschaft für Mineraloele mbH & Co v Petroplus Marketing AG (The Mercini Lady)* [2010] EWCA Civ 1145; [2011] 1 Lloyd's Rep. 442.

[2242B] See para.18–298A of this Supplement.

[2242C] [2010] EWCA Civ 1145 at [22].

(b)   *Consumer Sales*

Buyer dealing as consumer

[*fn.2251, line 1, after* "1 W.L.R. 321." *add*]   **18–302**
; contrast *Air Transworld Ltd v Bombardier Inc* [2012] EWHC 243 (Comm);
[2012] 1 Lloyd's Rep. 349, where the acquisition by a company of a private jet
for use by its controlling shareholder was held to be an "integral part of [the
company's] business" and so not to amount to a dealing by the company as
consumer (at [120]–[121]).

5.   IMPLIED TERMS

(a)   *Description*

Physical characteristics

[*Add at the end of fn.2352*]   **18–316**
    In *RG Grain Trade LLP v Feed Factors Ltd* [2011] EWHC 1889 (Comm),
[2011] 2 Lloyd's Rep. 432 an f.o.b. contract provided under the heading
"Commodity" that its subject-matter was "Ukrainian Origin Sunflower Expeller"
and under the heading "Specification" (*inter alia*) "Fiber max 23%" at [4]. Hamblen
J. held that the latter statement was not part of the description of the goods, as it did
not "appear next to the description of the goods. On the contrary, it appears under
the heading 'Specifications' and next to a specific characteristic which is clearly a
matter of quality rather than description, namely protein" (at [41]).

[*Add at the end of fn.2357*]
    For further discussion of *Tradax Internacional SA v Goldschmidt SA* [1977] 2
Lloyd's Rep. 604 and *Tradax Export SA v European Grain & Shipping Co* [1983]
2 Lloyd's Rep. 100, see the *RG Grain Trade* case, above fn.2352. Hamblen J. held
that the arbitration Board of Appeal had made a "clear error of law" in concluding
that there was a "right of rejection for quality matters unless the contract provided
otherwise" and in failing to consider "whether the fibre content provision should
properly be regarded as a condition, as opposed to a warranty or innominate term"
(at [42]). He remitted the case to the Board for determination of this issue (at [43]).

[*Add at the end of fn.2358*]
    In the *RG Grain Trade* case (above, fn.2352) the price adjustment clause of the
contract (set out at [5]) contained no reference to the fibre content of the goods:
see at [27].

(c)   *Non-rejection Clauses*

International supply contracts

[*fn.2416, line 2, after* "c.i.f. or f.o.b. terms'" *add*]   **18–324**

; for a similar statement that s.26(4)(a) of the Unfair Contract Terms Act 1977 "would apply to the sale of goods on cif or fob terms where the seller undertook to ship goods to, but not to deliver them at, any overseas destination", see *Air Transworld Ltd v Bombardier Inc* [2012] EWHC 243 (Comm); [2012] 1 Lloyd's Rep. 349 at [68]. As is pointed out in Main Work para.18–324 fn.2416, such an undertaking is by no means a necessary feature of an f.o.b. contract, since such a contract does not normally specify the destination of the goods

[*Add at the end of fn.2420*]
For the view that s.26(4)(a) of the Unfair Contract Terms Act 1977 applies "without any requirement in the contract for the seller to have undertaken an obligation in the contract to deliver the goods in any other state", see *Air Transworld Ltd v Bombardier Inc* [2012] EWHC 243 (Comm); [2012] 1 Lloyd's Rep. 349 at [68].

[*fn.2421, delete "At" and insert*]
[2009] EWCA Civ 290 at

[*Add new fn.2426A after "done"" 8 lines from the foot of p.1419*]

2426A For discussion of the question of where "the acts constituting the offer and acceptance have been done" within Unfair Contract Terms Act 1977 s.26(4)(b), see *Air Transworld Ltd v Bombardier Inc* [2012] EWHC 243 (Comm); [2012] 1 Lloyd's Rep. 349 at [68] *et seq.* Cooke J. there concluded at [82] that the phrase quoted above referred "to the totality of the acts which constitute the offer and acceptance including both the making and receiving of each." Accordingly, the requirements of s.26(4)(b) were satisfied where "the acts of sending and receipt of the offer took place in different states" (at [83]); and where this was also true of the acts of sending and receipt of the acceptance (*ibid.*).

[*fn.2432, line 2, add after "Sch.4)."*]
For an application of Unfair Contract Terms Act 1977, s.27(1), see *Transworld Ltd v Bombardier Inc* [2012] EWHC 243 (Comm); [2012] 1 Lloyd's Rep. 349, where English law was held at [101] to be the law governing the relevant contract "solely as a result of the express choice of law clause."

8.   SUPERVENING PROHIBITION OF EXPORT OR IMPORT

(a)   *Discharge by Supervening Prohibition*

Qualified prohibition

18–380   [*Add new fn.2784A after "discharged." in line 3 of the paragraph*]

2784A *Cf. Islamic Republic of Iran Shipping Lines v Steamship Mutual Underwriting Association of Bermuda* [2010] EWHC 2661 (Comm); [2011] 1 Lloyd's Rep. 195, where an Order issued under the Terrorism Act 2005 prohibited business relations without Treasury licence between persons operating in the financial sector (including the defendant insurer) and a class of persons including the claimant insurer. Licences were issued, the relevant one of which covered only specified classes of insurance. It was held that the insurance contract between these parties had not been frustrated by the combined effect of the Order and the restricted scope of the licences.

Partial prohibition

[*Add new fn.2793A after* "discharged" *in line 2 of the paragraph*]   **18–381**

2793A It will be apparent from the account of the *Islamic Republic of Iran Shipping Lines* case in para.18–380 of this Supplement that the supervening prohibition, together with the licences issued in pursuance of it, was not only "qualified" (in the sense explained in para.18–380 of the Main Work) but also partial. In the latter sense, these events did not frustrate the contracts since, although "the scope of the now permitted insurance is significantly narrower than it was before [the prohibition took effect], its nature is not different" (at [115], *per* Beatson J.).

CHAPTER 19

C.I.F. CONTRACTS

2. DUTIES OF THE SELLER

In general

[*Add at the end of fn.70*]   **19–010**
Paragraph 19–010 of the Main Work is cited with apparent approval in *Suek AG v Glencore International AG (The Hang Ta)* [2011] EWHC 1361 (Comm); [2011] 2 All E.R. (Comm) 1154 at [4].

(a)   *Shipment and Appropriation*

Notice of appropriation

[*Add at the end of fn.126*]   **19–017**
The decision in *Fortis Bank SA/NV v Indian Overseas Bank* [2009] EWHC 2303 (Comm); [2010] 1 Lloyd's Rep. 227 has been affirmed: [2011] EWCA Civ 58; [2011] 2 Lloyd's Rep. 33, where U.C.P. Art. 16(c) was said, as a matter of construction, to impose on a bank "an obligation to act in accordance with the notice" (at [36]), *i.e.* with a notice of the bank's decision to reject documents given under art.16.

(c)   *Tender of Documents*

Bad tender followed by good tender

[*fn.491, line 1, add after* "500."]   **19–072**
In *Buckland v Bournemouth University Higher Education Corporation* [2010] EWCA Civ 121; [2010] 4 All E.R. 186 the Court of Appeal held that an employer's repudiatory breach "once complete" (at [34]) could no longer be cured since, as a general principle of contract law "a completed breach, even if it can be compensated for, cannot be undone" (at [43]). These statements are not inconsistent with the rule stated in Main Work, para.19–072, to the effect that a seller who tenders defective documents within the shipment period is not thereby precluded from making another good tender, which the buyer is then obliged to accept, for until the end of the shipment period the seller's breach is not complete; and the rule does not in any event apply when the original bad tender can be (and is) accepted by the buyer as a repudiation of the contract.

3. DUTIES OF THE BUYER

(a)   *Payment of the Price*

Other payments to be made by buyer

[*Add at the end of fn.598*]   **19–089**

For an express provision making a c.i.f. buyer liable to the seller for demurrage, see also *Suek AG v Glencore International AG (The Hang Ta)* [2011] EWHC 1361 (Comm); [2011] 2 All E.R. (Comm) 1154 at [3]; for this case, see also para.19–090 of this Supplement.

[Add to text in line 21 after "charterparties."]
Another factor relevant to the question whether a demurrage provision in a sale contract operates by way of indemnity against the seller's liability to the carrier is whether the laytime provisions in the contract of sale "coincide"[607A] with those in the contract of carriage. In *Glencore Energy (UK) Ltd v Sonol Israel Ltd (The Team Anmaj),*[607B] for example, the fact that the contract of sale provided for laytime of 48 hours, while the charterparty to which that contract referred provided for laytime of 84 hours, was one reason for classifying the demurrage provision in the sale contract as one which did not operate by way of indemnity but gave rise to an "independent obligation."[607C] The same conclusion may also be based on the extent of the incorporation into the contract of sale of the charterparty provision: *e.g.* on the fact that the sale contract referred only to the "rate" of demurrage.[607D] The classification of a demurrage provision in a contract of sale as one giving rise to an "independent obligation" is also supported by the wider policy consideration that it promotes commercial certainty[607E] in that it enables the parties "to know precisely where they stand rather than to contract on a basis which makes their rights inter se depend upon the rights and liabilities of one of them [*i.e.* the seller] and possible disputes under some actual or future contract with a third party [*i.e.* the carrier]."[607F] Indeed, where the sale is on c.i.f. terms, even the seller may not be a party to the charterparty in question. His contractual relationship with the carrier may be only on bill of lading terms (either as an original party to the bill or, where goods are sold afloat, as a transferee of it); and then his liability for charterparty demurrage will depend on the effectiveness of a term in the bill of lading purporting to incorporate the charterparty demurrage term. Policy considerations analogous to the one mentioned above account for the reluctance of the courts to give effect to such incorporation terms.[607G]

[607A] *The Devon* (Main Work, para.19–089, fn.605) at [44].
[607B] [2011] EWHC 2756 (COMM), [2011] 2 Lloyd's Rep. 697.
[607C] *ibid.*, at [19] and [20].
[607D] *The Devon*, above, fn.607A at [45]; but *The Team Anmaj* (above, fn.607B) shows that the use of wider words (in that case, "Demurrage: As per charterparty rate, terms and conditions") will not necessarily lead to the conclusion that the demurrage provision in the sale contract operates by way of indemnity.
[607E] *The Team Anmaj*, above, fn.607B at [17].
[607F] *The Devon*, above, fn.607A at [33].
[607G] See *Miramar Maritime Corp v Holborn Oil Trading Ltd (The Miramar)* [1984] A.C. 767; *Carver on Bills of Lading* (3rd edn, 2011), para.3–038.

(b)   *Other Duties*

Other duties imposed by the contract

19–090   *[Add at the end of the text]*

A c.i.f. contract may also impose a duty on the buyer to provide a berth at the port of discharge[624A]; failure or delay in performing this duty may then make the buyer liable to the seller for demurrage.[624B]

[624A] *Suek AG v Glencore International AG (The Hang Ta)* [2011] EWHC 1361 (Comm), [2011] 2 All E.R. (Comm) 1154; it is submitted that the statement at [14] that "it is for the buyer to provide a berth" is not a general statement of the duties of a c.i.f. buyer, but merely reflects the express provision to this effect in cl.7.11 of the contract in that case, set out at [3].
[624B] See this Supplement, para.19–089.

4. CONTRACTUAL RELATIONS WITH CARRIER

Seller named as shipper

[fn.632, delete "See" and add]   **19–092**
See the reference to c.i.f. contracts in *TICC Ltd v Cosco (UK) Ltd* [2001] EWCA Civ 1862; [2002] CLC 347 at [17], cited in *Fortis Bank SA/NV v Indian Overseas Bank* [2011] EWHC 538 (Comm); [2011] 2 Lloyd's Rep. 190 at [62]. In the latter case, goods were shipped by a seller on CFR ("viz. Cost ad Freight": at [2]) terms under bills of lading naming the seller as shipper (at [7]) and the bank which had supplied the letter of credit issued in payment for the goods as consignee. It was held (at [62]–[67]) that the seller had not acted as the bank's agent in making the contract of carriage, so that the bank was not a party to the contract of carriage (and see this Supplement para.18–169 fn.1443). For further proceedings in this case, see [2011] EWCA Civ 58; [2011] 2 Lloyd's Rep. 33. *Cf.,*

[Add at the end of fn.632]
See also *Fortis Bank SA/NV v Indian Overseas Bank (No.2)* [2011] EWHC 538; [2012] 1 All E.R. (Comm) 41 where a seller of steel on "CFR" (or c & f: see this Supplement para.19–092 fn.632 and Main Work, para.21–012 fn.42) terms had shipped the goods under a bill of lading naming the seller as shipper and a bank (which had issued letters of credit to secure payment of the price) as consignee. It was held that, in so taking out the bill of lading, the seller had not acted as agent for the bank so as to make it a party to (and hence liable under) the contract contained in or evidenced by the bill of lading. The policy reason for this conclusion was that to hold the bank so liable would be "contrary to the regime of the 1992 [Carriage of Goods by Sea] Act" as it would "open banks up to potentially enormous liabilities" (at [67]; and *cf.* Main Work and this Supplement, para.18–170).

5. PASSING OF PROPERTY

In general

[Add at the end of fn.685]   **19–099**
Cf. Kulkarni v Manor Credit (Davenham) Ltd [2010] EWCA Civ 69; [2010] 2 All E.R. (Comm) 1017 where, on the sale of a car to a consumer who had paid the

price in full (at [2]), Rix L.J. said at [38] that there was "force in [the] submission" that "property [was] in general not intended to pass until delivery . . . at any rate where as here the contract is not for the sale of a specific car and the buyer has never seen the car." In that case, it was important for the purposes of s.27 of the Hire-Purchase Act 1964 for the consumer to establish that the passing or purported passing of property had taken place only after the seller to him had become the hirer of the car: see *ibid.*, at [16], [17].

8. REMEDIES OF THE BUYER

(a) *Rejection*

Qualifications

19–161   [*Add at the end of fn.1141*]
Thai Marparn Trading Co Ltd v Louis Dreyfus Commodities Asia Pte Ltd [2011] EWHC 2494 (Comm); [2011] 2 Lloyd's Rep. 704 at [24] (f.o.b. contract).

[*fn.1142, delete "ibid." and insert*]
[1954] 1 W.L.R. 1273 at p.1277.

[*Add at the end of fn.1145*]
See para.19–180 of this Supplement for the further discussion in *Acre 1127 Limited v De Montfort Fine Art Limited* [2011] EWCA Civ 85 of "estoppel or waiver" of the kind referred to at fn.1145 of para.19–161 of the Main Work.

19–173   [*fn.1245, add after* "at [269]–[272]."]
The decision in *Seadrill Management Services Ltd v OAO Gazprom (The Ekha)* [2009] EWHC 1530 (Comm); [2010] 1 Lloyd's Rep. 543 has been affirmed: [2010] EWCA Civ 1409; [2011] 1 All E.R. (Comm) 1077, where the appeal was "on limited grounds" (at [1]) and the decision turned solely on the construction of the contract.

Conduct of the buyer

19–180   [*Add at the end of fn.1307*]
See also the discussion of *Braithwaite v Foreign Hardwood Company* [1905] 2 K.B. 543 in *Acre 1127 Limited v De Montfort Fine Art Limited* [2011] EWCA Civ 85 at [51] and the citation there with approval of the statement of Sankey J. in *Cooper, Ewing & Co Ltd v Hamel & Horley Ltd* (1923) 13 Ll. L. Rep. 590 at 593 that "Braithwaite's case only lays down or reiterates a rule something in the nature of an estoppel or waiver . . .". In the *Acre* case (above) it was held that a prospective buyer could not recover damages in respect of an as yet unaccepted repudiation by the seller when the buyer was "neither ready nor willing to perform the contract itself and . . . did not seek further performance from [the seller]." The situation in the *Acre* case was said to be "analogous" to that discussed in cases such as *Braithwaite's* case, viz. that "a repudiating party has a defence to a claim in respect of that breach

by the innocent party if he can establish that, at the time of the repudiation, the innocent party was already irremediably disabled from performance, *provided that the
inability to perform on the part of the innocent party is not itself attributable to the
repudiatory breach*" (at [51]). The words here italicised in effect restate the principle
of "estoppel or waiver" referred to above in the *Cooper* case by Sankey J. who there
amplified that principle by saying that it "mean[t] no more than this, that, if one
person by an anticipatory breach of contract induces another person to whom he has
contracted not to complete the contract, the first person cannot be heard to say
subsequently that the second person is not ready and willing to perform it" ((1923)
13 Ll. L. Rep. 590 at 593). It is this principle of "inducement" which is put forward
in para.19–180 of the Main Work as one possible explanation of *Braithwaite*'s case.
The *Acre* case (above) extends that principle from cases in which the innocent party,
though not "irremediably disabled from performing", has made it clear that he "had
no intention of performing" ([2011] EWCA Civ 85 at [51]).

(b)   *Damages for Non-Delivery*

Other time designated by the contract

[*Add at the end of fn.1364*]   **19–190**
; *Thai Marparn Trading Co Ltd v Louis Dreyfus Commodities Asia Ltd* [2011]
EWHC 2494 (Comm), [2011] 2 Lloyd's Rep. 704 at [28] (f.o.b. contract), where
in view of the concession made by counsel for the sellers on the point, this issue
"f[e]ll away" (at [29]).

(c)   *Damages for Defective Delivery: in General*

(v)   *Analogy of Negligent Valuation Cases?*

Reasons for the decision in *The Achilleas*

[*Add at the end of fn.1528*]   **19–213**
For further discussion of the speeches in *Transfield Shipping Inc v Mercator
Shipping Inc (The Achilleas)* [2008] UKHL 48; [2009] 1 A.C. 61, see *Sylvia
Shipping Co Ltd v Progress Bulk Carriers Ltd (The Sylvia)* [2010] EWHC 542
(Comm); [2010] 2 Lloyd's Rep. 81 at [24] *et seq.* Hamblen J. in the latter case
concluded (at [40]) that "the orthodox approach [*i.e.* that "based on *Headley v
Baxendale*" (at [27])] remains the general test of remoteness applicable in the
majority of cases"; but that there might "be 'unusual' cases" (an apparent reference to Lord Hoffmann's speech in *The Achilleas* at [11]) in which "it is necessary
to consider whether there has been an assumption of responsibility." In *The Sylvia*
itself, *The Achilleas* was distinguished on the ground stated in para.19–218 of this
Supplement where the "orthodox approach" described above was applied and the
damages claimed were held not to be too remote.

[*Add at the end of fn.1528*]
In *Pindell Ltd v Air Asia Berhad* [2010] EWHC 2516 (Comm); [2011] 2 All
E.R. (Comm) 396 at [84] Tomlinson J. relied on the *Supershield* case [2010]
EWCA Civ 7; [2010] 1 Lloyd's Rep. 349 at [43] (cited in this note in the Main

Work), and on a number of decisions at first instance, in support of the view that the decision in *The Achilleas* [2008] UKHL 48; [2009] 1 A.C. 61 (Main Work, paras.19–212—19–219) had not "effected major changes in the approach to be adopted to the recoverability of damages for breach of contract".

19–218   [*Add at the end of fn.1577*]
     Transfield Shipping Inc v Mercator Shipping Inc (The Achilleas) [2008] UKHL 48; [2009] 1 A.C. 61 was distinguished in *Sylvia Shipping Co Ltd v Progress Bulk Carriers Ltd (The Sylvia)* [2010] EWHC 542 (Comm); [2010] 2 Lloyd's Rep. 81, where a time charterer claimed damages from the shipowner for loss suffered by reason of loss of a sub-charter occasioned by the owner's breach of the charter-party. The ground for the distinction was that the loss of the sub-charter was neither "completely unpredictable" (in the words of Lord Hope in *The Achilleas* quoted at this point in the Main Work) nor "completely unquantifiable" (in the words of Lord Hoffmann in that case quoted in para.19–218 at fn.1581 in the Main Work). The crucial difference between a claim for damages for loss of a follow-on charter (rejected in *The Achilleas*) and one for loss of a sub-charter (allowed in *The Sylvia*) was that a follow-on fixture "could be for any period" (*The Sylvia* at [73]), while "loss of a sub-charter during the currency of a time charter can never be for a longer period than the time charter itself" (*ibid.*). To this extent, too, the liability of the owner in respect of loss of a sub-charter is not, while the liability of the owner in respect of loss of a follow-on charter is (in the words of Lord Hope in *The Achilleas* quoted at fnn.1571 and 1582) "something over which they [*i.e.* the owners] had no control." In all these respects, the reasoning of *The Sylvia* seems to give some support to the submission made in para.19–218 of the Main Work, that the cases holding a c.i.f. seller liable for market loss damages (Main Work, paras 19–203—19–219) are not undermined by the reasoning of *The Achilleas*.

     [*Add at the end of fn.1578*]
     For another case in which the reasoning of *Transfield Shipping Inc v Mercator Shipping Inc (The Achilleas)* [2008] UKHL 48; [2009] 1 A.C. 1 was held not to apply, see *Transpetrol Maritime Services Ltd v SJB Maritime Energy BV (The Rowan)* [2011] EWHC 3374 (Comm); [2011] 2 Lloyd's Rep. 331, where a charterer recovered damages in respect of loss of a contract to sell a cargo to a specified buyer. It was said at [79] that "the loss was entirely foreseeable and there is no question of responsibility for it not having been assumed."

(e)   *Specific Performance and Injunction*

[*Insert new para.19–221A*]

Difficulty of enforcement

19–221A   In the case of an overseas sale by a foreign seller to an English buyer, practical difficulties of enforcement may also be a ground for refusing specific relief to the buyer. Thus where the goods were to be manufactured by a seller incorporated in a foreign country and having "no presence here",[1623A] and the acts which the seller was required to do in performance of the contract all had to be done in that country, a claim by the buyer for a mandatory injunction to secure delivery of the goods in this country was refused. One reason for this refusal was that such an injunction would "require an unacceptable degree of supervision [of the seller's perform-ance] in a foreign land"[1623B]; another was that it was "not apparent . . . how [such an order] could be enforced if it were broken" since "none of the traditional methods of enforcement would work."[1623C]

[1623A] *SSL International Plc v TTK LIG Ltd* [2011] EWHC 1695 (Ch) at [91], cited on appeal [2011] EWCA Civ 1170 at [85] and approved *ibid.*, at [95] and [97].
[1623B] *ibid.*, at [95]. The sale was not stated to be on c.i.f. terms, so that no question arose as to the place of tender of documents.
[1623C] [2011] EWHC 1695 (Ch) at [91], as to which see above, fn.1623A.

CHAPTER 20

F.O.B. CONTRACTS

2. DUTIES OF THE SELLER

(d) *Time of Shipment*

Express provision as to notice and rate of loading

20–035   *[Add at the end of fn.280]*
Bunge Corp v Tradax Export SA [1981] 1 W.L.R. 294 was distinguished and the part of the reasoning of that case summarised in para.20–034 of the Main Work was held to be inapplicable in *Thai Marparn Trading Co Ltd v Louis Dreyfus Commodities Asia Pte Ltd* [2011] EWHC 2494 (Comm); [2011] 2 Lloyd's Rep. 704. In that case, two contracts for the sale of rice on f.o.b. terms specified the shipment periods, and required the buyer to give "minimum 7 (seven) working days

written pre-advise [sic] of vessel's ETA" and also to serve a "notification of the vessel's readiness to load" (NOR). The buyer's notices given in pursuit of the first of these requirements gave the seller less than the stipulated seven days notice; and the seller argued that this fact amounted to a breach of condition (at [13]) or rendered the notice invalid (at [15]) so that the seller was not in breach by virtue of having made it clear that they would not have cargo available to load on the vessels nominated by the buyer under each of the two contracts. In rejecting these arguments, Beatson J. said that the notice of ETA was "of an 'estimated' time of arrival" (at [19]) and that there was "nothing in the contracts which suggests that the obligation to provide a cargo after tender of notice of readiness (triggering the running of lay time is dependent on first serving a notice giving seven working days notice of ETA" (at [19]). He also distinguished *Bunge Corp v Tradax Export SA* (above) on the ground that in that case "the breach consisted, not in giving less than the requisite number of days' notice but of giving notice after the last date on which it could be legitimately given because the required 15 days notice would have ended after the last possible date for shipment" (at [21]). The emphasis in this reasoning on the fact that the buyer was required by the contract of sale to give advance notice only of the *estimated* time of the vessel's arrival gives rise to the further question whether the outcome might have been different if the requirement had not been so qualified, *i.e.* if the buyer had been required simply to give seven days notice of the vessel's arrival at the port of loading. In that event, it would have been arguable that the stipulation formed part of a contractual scheme laying down a precise time-table for performance and should, for that reason, be classified as a condition (see Main Work, para.20–036 at fn.297); though the point made in the passage from [19], quoted above (*i.e.* that there was nothing in the contract to make the obligation to provide a cargo dependent on the giving of the notice) would still retain some force. The answer to this argument might well depend on the court's assessment of the purpose of requiring the buyer to give the notice. That purpose appears to be to give the seller some additional protection (going beyond the rule that the seller is bound to ship the goods only within a reasonable time of receiving the buyer's notice of the ship's readiness to load) against having to be able to ship the goods at any point during the shipment period (see Main Work, para.20–033), especially where that period is one of some length, as it was in the *Thai Marparn* case (above). An advance notice of the arrival of the ship gives the seller some chance of forecasting when that ship is likely to give notice of readiness to load; and that mitigation of the seller's duty with regard to having the goods ready for shipment at any time during the shipment period is obviously greater where the buyer's notice of the arrival of the ship has to specify a fixed, as opposed to a merely estimated, time. For this reason, it is arguable that there is a stronger case for treating the notice of arrival provision as a condition in the former, than in the latter, situation.

(e) *Conformity of the Goods*

Duty to ship conforming goods

[*Add at the end of fn.337*]   **20–042**
If the goods are in conformity with the contract at the time and place of shipment, the seller is not in breach merely because they are no longer in conformity with the

contract on arrival at the destination to which they have been carried in accordance with the buyer's shipping instructions: see *KG Bominflot Bunkergesellschaft für Mineraloele mbH & Co v Petroplus Marketing AG (The Mercini Lady)* [2010] EWCA Civ 1145; [2011] 1 Lloyd's Rep. 442, this Supplement para.18–298A. In that case, the seller's obligations as to quality and quantity were to be determined "basis shoretank", *i.e.* as Rix L.J. points out at [40] "not even on the basis of the gasoil in the [carrying] ship's tanks" and hence *before* shipment.

3. DUTIES OF THE BUYER

(a) *Shipping Instructions*

Shipping instructions must be "effective"

20–047   [*Add at the end of fn.370*]
Soufflet Nagoce v Bunge SA [2009] EWHC 2454 (Comm); [2010] 1 All E.R. (Comm) 1023 has been affirmed, *sub nom. Soufflet Negoce v Bunge SA* [2010] EWCA Civ 1102; [2011] 1 Lloyd's Rep. 531, where paras 20–046 and 20–047 of this book are referred to by Longmore L.J. at [9] with apparent approval and the buyers were held to have satisfied the contractual requirement of presenting the ship "in readiness to load within the delivery period" (see at [11]) even though the holds were at that time unclean (see at [6], [17]); for this purpose, the rules of charterparty law which determined when a valid "notice of readiness" had been given (for the purpose of running of lay time) did not apply between buyer and seller.

Time of shipment

20–050   [*Add at the end of fn.399*]
Soufflet Nagoce v Bunge SA [2009] EWHC 2454 (Comm); [2010] 1 All E.R. (Comm) 1023 has been affirmed, *sub nom. Soufflet Nagoce v Bunge SA* [2010] EWCA Civ 1102; see this Supplement para.20–047.

[*Add new fn.400A in line 16 after* "shipment period"]

400A An f.o.b. contract which gives the buyer an option to extend the shipment period is likely to require him to give notice of the extension to the seller, usually within a time specified in the contract. This was the position in *PEC Ltd v Thai Marparn Trading Co Ltd* [2012] 1 Lloyd's Rep. 295, where the notice given by the buyer was conditional on the sellers' within two days advising the readiness of cargo; and as "this never happened there was no valid claim for an extension" (at [18]).

[*Add at the end of fn.402*]
See also *Azimut-Benett SpA v Healey* [2010] EWHC 2234 (Comm), where a liquidated damages clause in a contract for the construction of a yacht was upheld as it was "commercially justifiable" (at [29]).

Time of shipment at buyer's option

[*Add new fn.407A after* "shipment period." *in line 12*]　　　　　**20–051**

407A For a recent statement of the f.o.b. buyer's duty "to nominate a ship at such time as will enable the seller to put the goods on board before the end of the shipment period", see *Kolmar Group AG v Traxpo Enterprises Pvt Ltd* [2010] EWHC 113 (Comm); [2010] 2 Lloyd's Rep. 653 at [105].

4.　Contractual Relations with Carrier

[*Insert new para.20–073A*]

Agent named as shipper

A further possibility is that the bill of lading may name as shipper a person who 　**20–073A** is neither the seller nor the buyer but is alleged to have taken out the bill of lading as agent for either the seller or the buyer, or for both of them. This possibility is illustrated by the *Maersk Line* case,[535A] where goods which had been sold on f.o.b. terms were shipped in China under a bill of lading which named the shipper as "B & D Co. Ltd. p/c (*pour compte de*) [an entity that was a subsidiary or associate of the buyer] and [the seller]".[535B] It was "not entirely clear"[535C] what this wording "was supposed to signify and in particular whether B & D was purporting to act as agent for both of them"[535D] but one "possible view" was that B & D had so acted: as agent for the buyer's subsidiary because it "appears to have paid the freight",[535E] and as agent for the seller since "by shipping the goods on board [the seller] had fulfilled its duties as f.o.b. seller".[535F] On this view, it was "possible for both seller and buyer to be party to the contract of carriage"[535G]; but no firm conclusion to this effect was reached since the relevant evidence was "in an unsatisfactory state".[535H] Christopher Clarke J. did indeed say that he "suspect[ed] that the correct analysis is that [the seller] participated in the contract evidenced by the . . . bill of lading at least to the extent of being entitled to exercise the right of the shipper to change the consignee . . ."[535I] These observations appear, however, to be *obiter*, the actual decision being that the seller was "entitled to the rights of the shipper"[535J] by virtue of a decision to that effect of a Chinese court, which had "never been set aside"[535K] and "made all the difference".[535L] This conclusion is also consistent with the Chinese court's view that the seller was (at the relevant time) owner[535M] of the goods—a view that is further consistent with that which would have been taken up by an English court as the buyer had not paid the price of the goods. As noted in para.20–009 of the Main Work, this fact would, in case of doubt, support the view that the seller was the shipper since such a view would be likely to give effect to the seller's intention as it would enable him to protect his security interest in the goods.

The further view, somewhat tentatively expressed, that the seller "participated in the contract evidenced by the . . . bill of lading"[535N] appears, in the first place, to be based on the assumption that the contract in which the seller "participated", and under which he therefore acquired rights, was the contract between carrier and buyer; and secondly to be derived from Devlin J.'s judgment in the *Pyrene Co Ltd v Scindia Navigation Co Ltd*,[535O] but, so far as one can tell from the report of the *Maersk Line* case, no attempt[535P] was there made to draw the attention of Christopher Clarke J. to the point that, in *Scruttons Ltd v Midland Silicones Ltd*,[535Q] Lord Simonds had said that the decision in the *Pyrene* case could be "supported only on the facts of the case which may well have justified the implication of a contract between the parties"[535R]: *i.e.* between carrier and seller, even though the contract of carriage was between carrier and buyer. Those (special) facts are set out in para.20–070 of the Main Work and seem to have no direct parallel with those of the *Maersk Line* case. That case is better regarded as one in which the seller was a principal party to the contract with the carrier, rather than as one in which the seller merely "participated" in a contract to which he was not a party.

[535A] *AP Moller-Maersk A/S (trading as Maersk Line) v Sonaec Villas Cen Sad Fadoul* [2010] EWHC 355 (Comm); [2010] 2 All E.R. (Comm) 1159 (hereafter "The *Maersk Line* case"). For further facts and issues in this case, see, para.18–200A of this Supplement.

[535B] [2010] EWHC 355 (Comm), at [6], [43].

[535C] *ibid.*

[535D] *ibid.*, at [43].

[535E] *ibid.*

[535F] *ibid.*

[535G] *ibid.*, at [47], perhaps referring back to [44].

[535H] *ibid.*, at [51].

[535I] *ibid.*

[535J] *ibid.*, at [52]. The syntax in the fourth and fifth sentences of [52] is a little obscure; probably the pronoun "it" refers to the entity called "High Goal"—not (as in the previous sentence) to the bill of lading.

[535K] *ibid.*

[535L] *ibid.*

[535M] See *ibid.*, at [12].

[535N] *Maersk Line* case, above fn.535A, at [51].

[535O] [1954] 2 Q.B. 402 at 426, quoted in the *Maersk Line* case, above fn.535A, at [45].

[535P] Perhaps because none of the defendants was represented.

[535Q] [1962] A.C. 446.

[535R] *ibid.*, at 471. In the *Midland Silicones* case, counsel for the defendants did not rely on the *Pyrene* case (above, fn.535O); Lord Simonds' explanation of the case appears to have been a response to the use made of that case by Lord Denning in his dissenting speech in the *Midland Silicones* case.

6. RISK

Generally passes on shipment

20–094   [*fn.682, line 11, after* "in the report." *add*]

Soufflet Nagoce v Bunge SA [2009] EWHC 2454 (Comm); [2010] 1 All E.R. (Comm) 1023 has been affirmed, *sub nom. Soufflet Negoce v Bunge SA* [2010] EWCA Civ 1102; see this Supplement, para.20–047. In the Court of Appeal, it was said at [8] that "the risk of loss or damage passed from the sellers to the buyers on the loading of the goods onto the vessel chartered by the buyers." See also *ibid.*, at [15], [17], [25].

Goods damaged or lost when being loaded

[*Add at the end of fn.698*]   **20–095**
See also the contractual provision for the passing of risk "on crossing ship's rail" under a CFR (*i.e.* c & f: see Main Work, para.21–012 fn.42) contract in *Fortis Bank SA/NV v Indian Overseas Bank* [2011] EWHC 538 (Comm); [2012] 1 All E.R. (Comm) 41 at [2].

9.   REMEDIES OF THE SELLER

(e)   *Rights against the Goods*

Seller's rights against the goods

[*Add at the end of fn.1036*]   **20–148**
The bailment reasoning at first instance in *ENE Kos v Petroleo Brasileiro SA (The Kos)* [2009] EWHC 1843 (Comm); [2010] 1 Lloyd's Rep. 86 (see Main Work, para.20–148 fn.1036) was rejected in the Court of Appeal ([2010] EWCA Civ 772 at [30]); but in the Supreme Court ([2012] UKSC 17) the shipowner's claim was upheld, not only on the construction of the charterparty, but also on the ground of a bailment that was "no longer contractual" (at [20]): see *per* Lord Sumption J.S.C. (with whom Lord Walker agreed) at [18]–[30], at [33] *per* Lord Phillips P. and at [57] *per* Lord Clarke.

CHAPTER 21

OTHER SPECIAL TERMS AND PROVISIONS IN OVERSEAS SALES

3. C. & F. Contracts

Duties of the parties

21–012 [*Add at the end of fn.42*]
For the usage referred to in Main Work, para.21–012 fn.42, see also *Fortis Bank SA/NV v Indian Overseas Bank* [2011] EWHC 538 (Comm); [2011] 2 Lloyd's Rep. 190 at [2] ("CFR CY . . . —viz Cost and Freight Container Yard").

8. Container Transport

(a) *Introductory*

Problems arising out of container transport

21–074 [*fn.472, line 4, after* "para.21–077)" *add*]
; *Carewins Development (China) Ltd v Bright Fortune Shipping Ltd* [2009] 1 HKLRD 409 at [7]; for this case, see this Supplement, para.18–097.

CHAPTER 22

NEGOTIABLE INSTRUMENTS IN OVERSEAS SALES

4.   DISCOUNT AND COLLECTION OF BILLS OF EXCHANGE

(a)   *Engagement of Banker*

[Delete existing para.22–069 and insert]   **22–069**

Discounting bank

Where a bank that has discounted a bill of exchange brings an action on the bill, an acceptor (or other party liable on the bill) is liable for the full face value of the bill, notwithstanding that the bank is liable to account to another party for a proportion of the amount of the bill once recovered. In principle, such liability of the bank does not afford the acceptor a *pro tanto* defence in the action on the bill.[190]

By way of exception, however, where the bank's liability is owed to the drawee, any defence available against the drawee had it retained the bills pending maturity is exercisable against the bank. In *Barclays Bank Ltd v Aschaffenburger Zellstoffwerke AG*,[191] the claimant bank discounted bills drawn by the seller on the buyer on terms that the bank would hold a proportion of the proceeds of the bills on trust for the seller. When the bank claimed on the bills for full value, it was held that, while judgment should be given in the full amount, there should be a stay of execution with respect to the proportion for which the bank was trustee for the seller pending resolution of a claim brought by the buyer against the seller.

[190] *GMAC Commercial Finance Ltd v Mint Apparel Ltd* [2010] EWHC 2452 (Comm).
[191] [1967] 1 Lloyd's Rep. 387. See also *Thornton v Maynard* (1875) L.R. 10 C.P. 695.

CHAPTER 23

DOCUMENTARY CREDITS

[At the beginning of fn.1 insert]   **23–001**
Quoted in *Ibrahim v Barclays Bank Plc* [2012] EWCA Civ 640 at [57].

3.   THE UNIFORM CUSTOMS AND PRACTICE FOR DOCUMENTARY CREDITS

[Change paragraph title to "**ICC guidance on interpretation**"*]*   **23–007**

[Change paragraph title to "**Status and applicability of the UCP**"*]*   **23–008**

[Lines 6–11, delete "Consistent with this . . . that the UCP applies."*]*

[Insert new para.23–008A]

Interpretation in law

Consistent with their contractual status, the provisions of the UCP fall to be   **23–008A**
construed in accordance with the normal approach to commercial contracts.[31A] At
the same time, regard must be had to the UCP's international character and its
purpose and function within the international trade finance system. In *Fortis Bank
SA/NV v Indian Overseas Bank (Nos 1 & 2)*,[31B] Thomas L.J. described the
approach to be adopted as follows:

"In my view, a court must recognise the international nature of the UCP and
approach its construction in that spirit. It was drafted in English in a manner
that it could easily be translated into about 20 different languages and applied
by bankers and traders throughout the world. It is intended to be a self-contained
code for those areas of practice which it covers and to reflect good practice and
achieve consistency across the world. Courts must therefore interpret it in
accordance with its underlying aims and purposes reflecting international practice and the expectations of international bankers and international trade. A
literalistic and national approach must be avoided."

Consequently, the opinions of the ICC Banking Commission,[31C] while not
conclusive, should be accorded due weight as evidence of international banking
practice.[31D] On the same basis, regard may be had to DOCDEX arbitration
awards.[31E]
On occasion, English courts have been persuaded of the need to acknowledge
an implied term in the UCP in accordance with orthodox common law principles.[31F]
The approach to interpretation of the UCP outlined by Thomas L.J., however,
mandates caution before courts of any one jurisdiction jeopardise the harmonisation achieved by the UCP by writing in new provisions in the form of terms
implied in accordance with any national law, as distinct from implication by way
of interpretation in accordance with the approach indicated above.[31G]

[31A] *Bankers Trust Co v State Bank of India* [1991] 2 Lloyd's Rep. 443 at p.456.
[31B] [2011] EWCA Civ 58; [2011] 1 C.L.C. 276 at [29]. See also *Glencore v Bank
of China* [1996] 1 Lloyd's Rep. 135 at p.148.

31C See above, para.23–007.

31D *Crédit Agricole Indosuez v Crédit Suisse First Boston* [2001] 1 All E.R. (Comm) 1088 at [23]. See also *Credit Industriel et Commercial v China Merchants Bank* [2002] EWHC 973 (Comm); [2002] C.L.C. 1263.

31E See, for example, *Fortis Bank SA/NV v Indian Overseas Bank (Nos 1 & 2)* [2011] EWCA Civ 58; [2011] 1 C.L.C. 276 at [34].

31F *Seaconsar Far East Ltd v Bank Markazi Jomhouri Islami Iran* [1999] 1 Lloyd's Rep. 36 at p.39. Or denied any implied term on the same principles: *Bankers Trust Co v State Bank of India* [1991] 1 Lloyd's Rep. 587 at p.599, reversed on grounds of interpretation rather than implication: [1991] 2 Lloyd's Rep. 443 (in so far as there is any distinction: *Attorney-General of Belize v Belize Telecom Ltd* [2009] UKPC 10; [2009] 1 W.L.R. 1988; *Mediterranean Salvage & Towage Ltd v Seamar Trading & Commerce Inc (The Reborn)* [2009] EWCA Civ 531; [2009] 1 C.L.C. 909).

31G *Fortis Bank SA/NV v Indian Overseas Bank (Nos 1 & 2)* [2011] EWCA Civ 58; [2011] 1 C.L.C. 276 at [55].

4. THE CONCEPT OF A DOCUMENTARY CREDIT

The issuing bank's undertaking

23–019   *[Add at the end of the text]*

The issuing bank's reimbursement obligation is owed only to the forwarding nominated bank, and it owes no obligation to the beneficiary where a nominated bank duly honours or negotiates. Consequently, where a confirming bank honoured, the issuing bank incurred no liability to the beneficiary for any loss caused by its wrongful refusal to reimburse.[82A]

82A *Fortis Bank SA/NV v Indian Overseas Bank (No.3)* [2011] EWHC 538 (Comm); [2012] 1 All E.R. (Comm) 41 at [37]–[38].

5. ESTABLISHING THE CREDIT

Application for issuance of a credit

23–027   *[Line 13, after "bank's preferred agent." add]*

Should the bank require any changes to terms of the credit stipulated in the underlying contract between the buyer and seller, the seller's consent to the amendment will need to be sought.

If the bank is prepared to issue the credit on the requested terms, it will . . .

[Add at the end of the text]

An issuing bank's standard terms may alternatively be incorporated by means of either a master agreement envisaging the issuing of a number of credits (on either an obligatory or facultative basis as far as the bank is concerned) within stated individual or aggregate limits or a more general agreement governing the bank's entire relationship with the applicant, including but not restricted to documentary credits.[107A]

^{107A} For an example of the latter, see *Petrologic Capital SA v Banque Cantonale de Genève* [2012] EWHC 453 (Comm).

Correspondent as advising bank

[*line 8, delete* "on that bank's behalf. Nevertheless, UCP 600 art.9 provides" **23–029**
and insert]
    or refuse the presentation on that bank's behalf. In such a case, the extent of the advising bank's authority to act on behalf of the issuing bank is not addressed by the UCP but depends on the application of the ordinary laws of agency.^{109A} UCP 600 art.9 does, however, provide

^{109A} *Seaconsar Far East Ltd v Bank Markazi Jomhouri Islami Iran* [1994] 1 A.C. 438 at p.457.

6.   Compliance of the Credit with the Underlying Contract

Condition precedent

[*Add at the end of fn.144*] **23–047**
    Under an FOB contract, the condition precedent is to the seller's duty to perform any part of the loading operation and therefore to the running of laytime under the sale contract (but not to the running of laytime under any relevant charterparty): *Kronos Worldwide Ltd v Sempra Oil Trading Sarl* [2004] EWCA Civ 3; [2004] 1 C.L.C. 136. See also *Glencore Grain Rotterdam BV v Lebanese Organisation for International Commerce* [1997] 2 Lloyd's Rep. 386 at p.394 *per* Evans L.J.: "Absent any special agreement, the sellers are entitled to see a conforming letter of credit in place before they begin shipment of the goods".

[*Add at the end of fn.146*]
    And see *Vitol SA v Conoil Plc* [2009] EWHC 1144 (Comm), [2009] 2 Lloyd's Rep. 466, in which an ex-ship contract expressly provided that opening the credit was a condition precedent to the seller's obligation to discharge the cargo and that failure to make the credit available to the seller by a specified date entitled the seller to terminate the contract and claim damages.

Strict nature of requirement to furnish credit

[*Add at the end of the text*] **23–048**
    Non-performance will, nevertheless, be excused where opening the credit would be illegal or contrary to public policy.^{147A}

^{147A} See, for example, *Soeximex SAS v Agrocorp International Pte Ltd* [2011] EWHC 2743 (Comm) (arbitration appeal based on sanctions legislation).

Shipment period (2): buyer in control of precise shipment date

[*Line 9, after* "is elusive." *add*] **23–053**

A rule based on the commencement of the shipment period is also unworkable where the contract is concluded after the period has commenced.[159A]

[159A] As in *Glencore Grain Rotterdam BV v Lebanese Organisation for International Commerce* [1997] 2 Lloyd's Rep. 386.

[*Delete third paragraph* ("If the relevant ... would be unreasonable.") *and insert*]

If the relevant date is, nevertheless, the first date of the shipment period, requiring the credit to be available a reasonable time before that date introduces the uncertainty discussed above.[159B] If, however, the relevant date is the actual shipment date as determined by the buyer and communicated to the seller in accordance with a contractual notice provision, it is arguable that the uncertainty disappears: the required notice of the nominated shipment date, perhaps in the form of notice of the carrying vessel's arrival at the port of loading, may be assumed, in the absence of contrary indication, to be the time required by the seller to prepare for timely loading and to represent the duration of advance financial reassurance that would be reasonable. The persuasiveness of this argument is, however, weakened by the variety of notice provisions that may be found in FOB contracts. Where, for example, the contract provides for a first provisional notice to be followed by a final notice,[159C] it is not immediately obvious which notice period would be relevant for documentary credit purposes. There is considerable merit in any default rule being clear. While there may be room for debate whether the terms of a particular contract displace a default rule, it is preferable that the operation of the default rule itself does not depend on the true interpretation of the contract. On this basis, a rule that, where the buyer controls the precise shipment date, the credit needs to be open prior to the date when loading should commence is preferable.

[159B] Above, para.23–052.
[159C] See *Cargill UK Ltd v Continental UK Ltd* [1989] 2 Lloyd's Rep. 290.

Ian Stach

23–056   [*Delete second and third paragraphs and insert*]

It is, however, respectfully submitted that the reference to string trading is misplaced. That a particular transaction forms part of a string cannot, in the abstract and even assuming both parties are aware there is a string, determine when a credit needs to be available. Where each credit in a series is opened on the strength of the credit that directly funds the next link down the string, the opening dates of the various credits will necessarily be staggered. Adopting a single opening date of the commencement of the shipment period is, therefore, impossible; yet a reasonable time before then is dependent on the position of the relevant transaction in the string, which, as Diplock J. notes, is something any particular buyer cannot be expected to know.

On the facts of *Ian Stach*, it was unnecessary to decide which of the sellers' contentions was correct, and Diplock J. confined himself to holding that the credit had to be open by the commencement of the shipment period "at the latest", but it is hard to see why, on the reasoning of Diplock J., assessing a reasonable time before the commencement of the shipment period would be any more certain than assessing a reasonable time before the actual shipment date. On that basis, the case may be read as favouring opening by the commencement of the shipment period.[164] Of course, where the buyer calls for shipment at the beginning of that period such a rule denies the seller any possibility of acting in reliance on the credit, a commercial desire to which Diplock J. was sympathetic but that cannot be accommodated without the introduction of unacceptable uncertainty.

[164] This view is seemingly accepted by Lloyd J. in *State Trading Corp of India v Compagnie Française d'Importation et de Distribution* [1983] 2 Lloyd's Rep. 679 at p.680, but the case turned on the interpretation of a requirement that the credit be opened "immediately": see para.23–050. See also *Glencore Grain Rotterdam BV v Lebanese Organisation for International Commerce* [1997] 2 Lloyd's Rep. 386 at p.393; *Kolmar Group AG v Traxpo Enterprises Pvt Ltd* [2010] EWHC 113 (Comm); [2010] 1 C.L.C. 256 at [102]–[104].

Conclusions

[*line 11, delete* "Where the buyer controls . . . by the time such notice is given." **23–057**
and insert]
Where the buyer controls the precise shipment date, it is difficult to formulate a default rule by reference to a reasonable time before the relevant date without introducing undesirable uncertainty. The case law accordingly favours a fixed date rule, the date being the commencement of the shipment period. There appears to be no reason, however, why the buyer should be placed in repudiatory breach by failing to provide the seller with assurance of payment by a date that has no sensible connection with the timetable for contractual performance. Moreover, resort to the favoured rule is precluded where the contract is concluded after the commencement of the shipping date. It is, therefore, suggested that a rule that ties the obligation to make a conforming credit available to the seller to the date on which the seller is required to commence loading is more congruent with FOB contracts.

Credit at variance with the terms of the contract

[*line 11, after* "seller's shipment obligations." *insert new fn.182A*] **23–062**

[182A] For example, *Kolmar Group AG v Traxpo Enterprises Pvt Ltd* [2010] EWHC 113 (Comm); [2010] 1 C.L.C. 256 at [108]–[109].

7. Two Fundamental Principles: Irrevocability and Autonomy

(b) *The Autonomy of Documentary Credits*

[*fn.215, delete existing text and insert*] **23–070**
See also below, para.23–073.

[*line 13: after* "may have against the applicant" *insert*]
are not affected by and

[*fn.216, delete existing text and insert*]
Société Générale SA v Saad Trading [2011] EWHC 2424 (Comm); [2011] 2
C.L.C. 629 at [33]–[34]. See also *Petrologic Capital SA v Banque Cantonale de
Genève* [2012] EWHC 453 (Comm) (applicant unable to invoke Contracts (Rights
of Third Parties) Act 1999 in order to claim benefit of jurisdiction clause in the
credit in its relationship with the issuing bank). The same applies in respect of rights
the issuing bank may not have against the applicant. Thus, that the insolvency of the
applicant prejudices the issuing bank's prospects of reimbursement is irrelevant to
the issuing bank's obligations under the credit: *McNeil Electronics Ltd v American
Sensors Electronics Inc* (1998) 39 O.R. (3d) 32. On the applicant-issuing bank
relationship, see further above, para.23–027.

[*fn.217, delete existing text and insert*]
Quoted in *Ibrahim v Barclays Bank Plc* [2012] EWCA Civ 640 at [60].

Independence from the underlying contract

23–071   [*Add at the end of fn.218*]
Autonomy thus precludes any assistance being gained as to the governing law
or jurisdiction of the credit from choice of law or jurisdiction clauses in the underlying contract: *Attock Cement Co Ltd v Romanian Bank for Foreign Trade* [1989]
1 W.L.R. 1147. With respect, conversely, to clauses in the credit influencing the
governing law and jurisdiction of the underlying contract, it is clear that (1) the
credit cannot override express terms in the underlying contract, and (2) autonomy
is no impediment. Whether the general transactional context militates against
such influence is debatable: *Petrologic Capital SA v Banque Cantonale de Genève*
[2012] EWHC 453 (Comm) at [47]–[48]. On private international law issues, see
further below, para.26–087.

Express restrictions in the underlying contract

23–078   [*fn.239, after* "[2003] 1 W.L.R. 2214" *insert*]
; *Simon Carves Ltd v Ensus UK Ltd* [2011] EWHC 657 (TCC); [2011]
B.L.R. 340

8.   TIME AND PLACE OF PRESENTATION

[*Insert new para.23–086A*]

Contractual presentation requirement

23–086A   The credit can, of course, establish a different temporal restriction. Thus, a
provision that presentation is to be "within 21 days from B/L date" clearly requires
presentation within 21 days of the date of issue of the bill of lading irrespective of
the date of shipment. Article 14(c) is displaced.[266A]

^{266A} *Fortis Bank SA/NV v Indian Overseas Bank (Nos 1 & 2)* [2011] EWCA Civ 58; [2011] 1 C.L.C. 276 at [71]–[77].

Extension of the last date for presentation

[*line 10, after* "by such a matter of *force majeure.*" *insert new fn.267A*]   **23–087**

^{267A} Contrast the extensions afforded under uniform rules governing autonomous guarantees: below, para.24–036.

9.   REALISATION OF A DOCUMENTARY CREDIT

Examination of presented documents

[*line 15, after* "refusing a presentation." *insert new fn.274A*]   **23–092**

^{274A} The view expressed in the text was queried in *Société Générale SA v Saad Trading* [2011] EWHC 2424 (Comm); [2011] 2 C.L.C. 629 at [37]–[43] where it was considered that UCP 600 distinguished between presentation of documents by the beneficiary and forwarding from a presentee bank that has honoured or negotiated to either the issuing or confirming bank. Although it was not necessary to decide the point (this aspect of the case concerned rather whether the documents required to be forwarded in support of a reimbursement claim included bills of exchange, as to which see below, para.23–225A), it was suggested that arts 14–16 might refer only to the processing of documents presented by the beneficiary and not to the processing of documents received by way of a claim for reimbursement. It is submitted, however, that such doubts as to the applicability of arts 14 and 16 are misplaced (art.15 admittedly does not speak to reimbursement) and that the view stated in the text (in this paragraph and para.23–219) is correct for the following reasons.

First, if arts 14 and 16 do not apply, the UCP will be silent on the obligations of the reimbursing bank with respect to processing the documents. In default of any express stipulation, the only obligation will be to process within a reasonable time, and the inapplicability of art.16(c) will leave the commercial imperative of certainty as to the fate of the documents dependent upon the unreliable beneficence of implied terms. When contrasted with the clarity and strictness of the obligations undertaken towards the beneficiary by a nominated bank (especially a confirming bank, which is subject to the sanction of preclusion), such vagueness in the reimbursement regime is, it is suggested, both commercially unacceptable and a highly improbable interpretation of an international commercial instrument.

Secondly, the suggested distinction between forwarding and presentation relies on a narrow interpretation of "presentation" that the relevant definitions in UCP 600 art.2, not referred to in *Société Générale*, do not support. "Presentation" is defined as including "the delivery of documents under a credit to the issuing bank or nominated bank", wording that is sufficiently broad to include delivery by a beneficiary seeking payment or delivery by a paying bank in support of reimbursement. Moreover, a broad reading is supported by the definition of "presenter", which embraces "a beneficiary, bank or other party that makes a presentation". If, however, nominated banks (including confirming banks) seeking reimbursement are excluded, it is extremely difficult to do justice to the breadth of this definition. Consequently, it is suggested that the applicability of certain additional provisions in arts 7(c) and 8(c) to forwarding by way of claiming reimbursement does not detract from the proposition that such forwarding, nevertheless, involves a presentation and the full applicability of arts 14 and 16.

Thirdly, it has never previously been doubted in the case law that the UCP rules as to the processing of documents apply to both presentations for payment and presentations for reimbursement. Admittedly, the issue has not been expressly addressed, but it is suggested that on this point silence is eloquent. Otherwise the litigation in, for example, *Bankers Trust Co v State Bank of India* [1991] 1 Lloyd's Rep. 587, [1991] 2 Lloyd's Rep. 443 (UCP 400), *Bayerische Vereinsbank Aktiengesellschaft v National Bank of Pakistan* [1997] 1 Lloyd's Rep. 59 (UCP 500), and most recently, *Fortis Bank SA/NV v Indian Overseas Bank (Nos 1 & 2)* [2009] EWHC 2303 (Comm); [2009] 2 C.L.C. 550; [2010] EWHC 84 (Comm); [2010] 1 C.L.C. 16; affirmed [2011] EWCA Civ 58; [2011] 1 C.L.C. 276 and *Fortis (No.3)* [2011] EWHC 538 (Comm); [2012] 1 All E.R. (Comm) 41 (UCP 600) has all been based on a fundamental misconception. It is true that successive revisions of the UCP have seen significant changes in drafting, but, as demonstrated by *Fortis*, arguments that a drafting change imports a change in substance that runs counter to commercial sense will be rejected.

10. COMPLIANCE: GENERAL PRINCIPLES

Appearance of presented documents on their face

23–098   *[Insert new second paragraph in text after fn.313]*

In *Fortis Bank SA/NV v Indian Overseas Bank (Nos 1 & 2)*,[313A] a beneficiary's certificate attested that the negotiating bank had been advised to forward documents by courier at the issuing bank's expense instead of, as required by the credit, at the beneficiary's cost. In fact, the forwarding charges were paid by the beneficiary, and it was argued that the disparity between the certificate and the credit should be overlooked as an obvious error that would be known to the bank because it had not engaged the courier or paid any charge on delivery. This argument was rejected:

> "Even if this were known to someone in IOB [the issuing bank], those checking the documents (including management supervising them) would not have known this; they could not have discerned this from the documents and they were under no obligation to make enquiries of others within IOB as to whether IOB had engaged the courier or paid the courier."[313B]

[313A] [2011] EWCA Civ 58; [2011] 1 C.L.C. 276.
[313B] At [19], *per* Thomas L.J.

Typographical errors

[*Add at the end of fn.321*]   **23–100**
A misspelling in the title of the document does not constitute a discrepancy as
evidently resulting from typographical error where it in no way compromises the
nature of the document, as attested by its content: *Collected Opinions 1995–2001*,
R 442 (Ref. 145) ("Certificate of Completition of Shop Testing").

[*fn.322. Delete* "would" *and insert*]
may

De minimis

[*fn.331, delete* "In *Seaconsar Far East* . . . specifically requires"]   **23–101**

[*Add at the end of fn.333*]
A one digit error in a six digit telex number has likewise been dismissed as
trivial: *Seaconsar Far East Ltd v Bank Markazi Jomhouri Islami Iran* [1993] 1
Lloyd's Rep. 236 at p.240.

Non–disparities

[*Line 7, after* "contract number", *replace full stop with comma, retain fn.336,*   **23–102**
and add]
or where "Ltd" is used instead of "Limited".[336A]

[336A] *Collected Opinions 1995–2001*, R 455 (Ref. 186). But omission altogether of
wording to the effect of "Limited" would constitute a discrepancy: *ibid.*

[*Line 7, delete* "Again," *and insert* "Greater difficulty arises where" *and start
new paragraph*]

[*At the end of the text, after fn.337, add*]
In *Seaconsar Far East Ltd v Bank Markazi Jomhouri Islami Iran*,[337A] however,
it was held that a failure to comply in respect of one tendered document with
a credit requirement to include the letter of credit number in all such documents
rendered the presentation discrepant. It was argued that the function of the
number was merely to establish linkage (as to which see para.23–124), a function
that was fulfilled by other information in the relevant document. This argument
was rejected by a majority of the Court of Appeal on the basis that an express
requirement for inclusion of the number had to be complied with in its own right
irrespective of the purpose behind its inclusion, as to which it was not permissible
to speculate. It does not appear to have been argued that inclusion of the letter of
credit number was required purely for the convenience of the bank and formed no
part of the conditions on which the bank was authorised by the applicant to accept
or reject a presentation. The credit, moreover, incorporated the 1983 revision of
the UCP and, therefore, pre-dated the qualifying of the concept of compliance by

reference to international standard banking practice, as reflected by the approach of the ICC Banking Commission.

337A [1993] 1 Lloyd's Rep. 236.

[*Insert new para.23–106A*]

Inappropriate credit terms

23–106A   A credit may contain a documentary requirement that is commercially incompatible with the underlying commercial relationship. However, that in practice compliance with a term of the credit is not feasible or realistic affords a bank no licence unilaterally to waive or amend the requirement; the autonomy principle precludes a bank from having regard to the underlying relationship between applicant and beneficiary.354A An amendment to the credit should be sought involving the consent of the applicant, beneficiary and participating banks.

354A *Swotbooks.com Ltd v Royal Bank of Scotland Plc* [2011] EWHC 2025 (QB) at [24].

Original documents

23–108   [*line 16, delete* "Moreover, the Decision" *and insert*]
The Decision itself

Relationship between stipulated documents

23–115   [*line 7, after* "but also "any other stipulated document"." *insert*]
Accordingly, the presentation was non-compliant where the presented invoice referred to a number of transport documents individually numbered, but only one document was presented as a transport document.397A

397A *Swotbooks.com Ltd v Royal Bank of Scotland Plc* [2011] EWHC 2025 (QB) at [27].
[*Continue existing text* ("As already discussed, . . .") *as new paragraph*]

[*After* "As already discussed" *insert new fn.397B*]

397B Above, para.23–113.

Quantity of goods

23–125   [*line 7, after* "permitted." *insert new fn.445A*]

445A But a barrel of crude oil is obviously a unit of measurement and not a packing unit.

"To be accepted as presented"

23–128   [*Delete existing title and insert*]

Deemed compliance clauses

The possibility of non-compliance creates a risk of non-payment for the beneficiary and non-reimbursement for a bank that has erroneously honoured the credit or negotiated. Clauses may be included in the credit or the issuing bank's application form aimed at eliminating this risk. A clause in the credit may deem the presented documents to comply with the terms and conditions of the credit, thus rendering the bank liable to pay the beneficiary and be entitled to reimbursement by any presentation purportedly under the credit. The same entitlement to reimbursement, although not conferring any rights on the beneficiary, results from a term in the issuing bank's application form that authorises the bank to pay against any presentation that purports to be made under the credit and provides that the fact that a payment is made shall be conclusive evidence of the bank's liability to pay under the credit.[456A] However, the promise of payment under a documentary credit once made may be autonomous, but it is procured in the context of the underlying contract in order to discharge an obligation under that contract to pay the other party for performance and on the basis that payment will be made only against documentary evidence of due performance. A deemed compliance clause denies this fundamental commercial understanding of a documentary credit and, consequently, invites the strictest of scrutiny with respect to both interpretation and validity.

[456A] See the issuing bank's application form in *Swotbooks.com Ltd v Royal Bank of Scotland Plc* [2011] EWHC 2025 (QB) at [7].

[Existing text becomes second paragraph]

[After existing text, insert new third paragraph]
More fundamentally, a deemed compliance term incorporated pursuant to the issuing bank's written standard terms of business into either the credit or the contract between the applicant and the issuing bank in order to safeguard reimbursement could not, it is suggested, absent compelling evidence that the clause represented the genuine intentions of the applicant, withstand challenge by the applicant under s.3 of the Unfair Contract Terms Act 1977 as a term that unreasonably entitles the bank "to render a contractual performance substantially different from that which was reasonably expected".[458A]

[458A] Pleaded but not relied upon at trial in *Swotbooks.com Ltd v Royal Bank of Scotland Plc* [2011] EWHC 2025 (QB): see [55]. A deemed compliance clause would be subject to the same challenge by the applicant.

11.   COMPLIANCE: SPECIFIC DOCUMENTS

(a)   *Commercial Invoice*

Commercial invoice

[line 7, after "of the credit", replace full stop with comma and insert] **23–131**
there being no basis on which to determine the appropriate exchange rate.[467A]

467A *Swotbooks.com Ltd v Royal Bank of Scotland Plc* [2011] EWHC 2025 (QB) at [35]–[36].

[*Add at the end of the text*]
There is no requirement concerning the date of issue of an invoice. In particular, there is no required temporal link with the transaction to which it relates. Consequently, a beneficiary can revise an invoice, or issue a fresh invoice in a similar or different form from the earlier version.474A

474A *Swotbooks.com Ltd v Royal Bank of Scotland Plc* [2011] EWHC 2025 (QB) at [30].

(b) *Transport Documents*

Introduction

23–132   [*line 8, after fn.475, add*]
A requirement for an otherwise unspecified transport document calls for a document that, at a minimum, evidences, first, receipt of the goods, including place and date, by the carrier for delivery to a specified consignee and, secondly, the terms of the contract of carriage pursuant to which the carrier will transport and deliver.475A

475A *Swotbooks.com Ltd v Royal Bank of Scotland Plc* [2011] EWHC 2025 (QB) at [18]–[21].

[*line 9, delete* "must" *and insert*]
need

(iii) *Bills of Lading*

Shipment

23–143   [*Add at the end of fn.503*]
A bill of lading that provides that any on board notation "shall be deemed to mean on board" the inland conveyance from the place of receipt of the goods to the port of loading cannot comply with art.20: Opinion TA679. See generally, "Recommendations of the Banking Commission in respect of the requirements for an On-board Notation" (2010).

13.   PRESENTATION CONSIDERED NON-COMPLYING

Mode of giving a notice of refusal

23–178   [*Insert at the beginning of fn.607*]
Seaconsar Far East Ltd v Bank Markazi Jomhouri Islami Iran [1997] 2 Lloyd's Rep. 89 at p.93;

Compliance with a refusal notice

[*Line 5, delete* "art.16 or by way of implied term, either analysis" *and insert*]
art.16(c),

[*Line 6, before* "expectations" *insert*]
commercial

[*fn.639, delete* "[2010] EWHC . . . C.L.C. 16." *and insert*]
(Nos 1 & 2) [2011] EWCA Civ 58; [2011] 1 C.L.C. 276.

[*Add at the end of the text*]
The presenter of the documents may respond to a refusal notice stating that the documents will be returned by disputing the bank's conclusion of non-compliance and demanding that the bank retains the documents and pays. Such a response will entitle the bank to retain the documents in contradiction of its refusal notice only if it accepts the presenter's demand in full and agrees to accept the documents and pay. The refusal notice is then rescinded by mutual consent.[639A]

[639A] *Fortis Bank SA/NV v Indian Overseas Bank (Nos 1 & 2)* [2011] EWCA Civ 58; [2011] 1 C.L.C. 276 at [68].

Time for returning documents

[*Delete existing text and footnotes and insert*]
As stated above, when a refusing bank espouses option (a) in its refusal notice or it espouses option (b) and the presenter subsequently instructs return, as a matter of the true interpretation of art.16(c) the bank comes under an obligation to return the documents to the presenter, an obligation, moreover, that must be fulfilled with reasonable promptness and without delay.[640] The precise amount of time thereby denoted should reflect the purely administrative nature and simplicity of the task in comparison with the examination of documents, determination of non-compliance and giving of a notice of refusal, for which the UCP allows a maximum of five banking days following the day of presentation. It should also acknowledge the need to prioritise the return of documents in order to prevent commercial paralysis resulting from the unavailability of the documents to the party with a trading interest in the goods to which they refer. An obligation to act with reasonable promptness is, nevertheless, not an obligation to act immediately and imports a degree of flexibility that acknowledges the severe consequence of non-compliance.[641] It has, accordingly, been held that a bank that failed to despatch the documents within three banking days of giving the notice of refusal would have failed to act with reasonable promptness.[641A]

[640] *Fortis Bank SA/NV v Indian Overseas Bank (Nos.1&2)* [2011] EWCA Civ 58; [2011] 1 C.L.C. 276 at [31]–[35].
[641] *Fortis Bank SA/NV v Indian Overseas Bank (No.2)* [2010] EWHC 84 (Comm); [2010] 1 C.L.C. 16 at [72]–[75]; *Fortis Bank SA/NV v Indian Overseas Bank (No.3)* [2011] EWHC 538 (Comm); [2012] 1 All E.R. (Comm) 41 at [32]–[34].

641A *Fortis Bank SA/NV v Indian Overseas Bank (No.3)* [2011] EWHC 538 (Comm); [2012] 1 All E.R. (Comm) 41 at [35]. A stricter general expectation of within one or two banking days was suggested in *Fortis Bank SA/NV v Indian Overseas Bank (No.2)* [2010] EWHC 84 (Comm); [2010] 1 C.L.C. 16 at [76].

Condition of returned documents

23–184   [*Add at the end of fn.643*]

This point was left open on appeal. The issuing bank sought to justify failure to return documents on the ground that the presenter's instruction to return after endorsement was invalid since there was no right to require re-endorsement. The Court of Appeal held, however, that such an instruction was effective at least as an instruction to return documents. Even if the issuing bank's contention regarding re-endorsement was correct, the documents should have been returned unendorsed: [2011] EWCA Civ 2011; [2011] 1 C.L.C. 276 at [70].

Failure to handle documents in accordance with the notice of refusal

23–190   [*Delete existing text and footnotes and insert*]

As previously discussed,656 a bank that issues a refusal notice is obliged to act in accordance with its terms, except for the licence granted by art.16(e) to return at any time documents that it has said it would continue to hold. Moreover, since this obligation arises on the true interpretation of art.16(c), a failure to act in accordance with the terms of a refusal notice will constitute a failure to act in accordance with the provisions of art.16 and will incur preclusion.657

656 Above, para.23–182.

657 *Fortis Bank SA/NV v Indian Overseas Bank (Nos 1 & 2)* [2011] EWCA Civ 58; [2011] 1 C.L.C. 276 at [36]–[45]. Consequently, the change in wording between UCP 500, art.14(e), which expressly applied preclusion to a failure to act in accordance with a refusal notice and UCP 600, art.16(f), which contains no such statement, is of no import. For preclusion following a failure to handle documents in accordance with a refusal notice under UCP 500, see, for example, *Unpublished Opinions 1995–2004*, R 546 (Ref. 350) (preclusion under UCP 500 followed when issuing bank rejected documents, stating they were held at the presenter's disposal, but then released three of them to the applicant); *Bayerische Vereinsbank Aktiengesellschaft v National Bank of Pakistan* [1997] 1 Lloyd's Rep. 59 at p.70.

Re-presentation of documents

23–194   [*line 5, after* "art.14" *delete* ", and, should". *Insert full stop and the following text*]

In particular, any modified or replacement document must be considered on its face and not by comparison with the previously presented version.663A Should . . .

[663A] *Swotbooks.com Ltd v Royal Bank of Scotland Plc* [2011] EWHC 2025 (QB) at [32].

16.   REIMBURSEMENT OF A NOMINATED BANK

Undertakings in the credit to reimburse

'[*line 4, after* "issuing bank." *insert new fn.721A*]   **23–218**

[721A] The issuing bank's reimbursement obligation is owed only to a nominated bank; it does not also promise the beneficiary that it will reimburse the nominated bank: see above, para.23–019.

Time for effecting reimbursement

[*line 13, after* "in accordance with art.16." *insert new fn.721B*]   **23–219**

[721B] See above, para.23–092.

Forwarding of documents

[*line 21, after* "indeed complied" *insert*]   **23–225**
and that the presented documents were indeed forwarded

[*Insert new para.23–225A*]

Forwarding of documents and bills of exchange

Where a credit calls for presentation of a bill of exchange, do the documents that require forwarding under UCP 600 arts 7(c) and 8(c) include the bill? Three situations involving presentation of a bill of exchange may be distinguished. First, the credit may require presentation of a bill drawn on the applicant, but a credit should not be issued available by such a bill[735A] since the applicant would otherwise be able to frustrate the fundamental purpose of a credit, namely to facilitate payment, by refusing to honour the bill. Such a bill may, therefore, be required to be presented and forwarded in the same manner as a commercial document, but it should not be the vehicle for payment under the credit. Secondly, where the credit is available by negotiation, it may be made available by acceptance of a bank other than the negotiating bank.[735B] In such a case, the required bill will have to be retained by the negotiating bank for presentation by that bank in turn to the drawee bank. Thirdly, the bill of exchange may be presented as an operative financial instrument, for acceptance by the presentee bank. Once accepted, the bill may be retained by the presenter pending presentment for payment on maturity, with an action of the bill available in case of dishonour. Alternatively, the presenter may exploit the negotiable nature of the bill in order to obtain accelerated receipt of disposable funds by procuring the discounting of the bill either by the accepting bank itself or by a different bank.   **23–225A**

Some difficulty may arise where the credit refers to bills of exchange drawn on a bank as "documents", but such bills should not be confused with the required commercial documents evidencing performance of the underlying contract. In particular, bills are not documents to which UCP 600 arts 7(c) and 8(c) speak, as require forwarding by the presentee bank to the issuing or confirming bank in order to trigger the reimbursement obligation of those banks. When presented for acceptance, the bills are the vehicle and receptacle for payment; they are no more documents than a leather bag required by the credit into which gold sovereigns are to be placed for taking away. Without the bills, the credit cannot be realised: the value to which the beneficiary is entitled by reason of making a compliant presentation cannot be made available to the beneficiary. However, to require the bills to be retained by the accepting bank for forwarding denies the entire commercial purpose of obtaining the acceptance of a bill of exchange. So to interpret a credit cannot, it is suggested, be consistent with the intentions of the parties as reasonable commercial traders and bankers, to give effect to which the credit, like any contract, should be interpreted.[735C]

[735A] ISBP 2007 para.54.
[735B] Above, para.23–161.
[735C] It is, accordingly, suggested that contrary dicta in *Société Générale SA v Saad Trading* [2011] EWHC 2424 (Comm); [2011] 2 C.L.C. 629 are incorrect.

Mistaken reimbursement

23–243   *[Add at the end of fn.778]*
See also *Swotbooks.com Ltd v Royal Bank of Scotland Plc* [2011] EWHC 2025 (QB) at [49]–[54].

[fn.778, delete "Cantrave" and insert]
Crantrave

[Add at the end of fn.779]
; *Ibrahim v Barclays Bank Plc* [2012] EWCA Civ 640.

17.   CREDIT FAILURE AND THE BENEFICIARY

Damages and the autonomy principle

23–252   *[line 4, after "presentation tendered," insert new fn.798A]*

[798A] Refusal will be wrongful either where the presentation is in truth compliant or where the bank is precluded from relying on any discrepancies that are present.

[Insert new para.23–252A]

Refusal wrongful by preclusion

A bank's refusal of a discrepant presentation will be wrongful where it incurs **23–252A**
preclusion in respect of the discrepancies. In such a case, the bank's breach of
obligation occurs at the time when preclusion is incurred. Where a bank fails to
give a notice of refusal, this occurs at the expiry of permitted time for giving a
notice, namely at the expiry of the fifth banking day following the day of receipt
of the documents. Where it gives a notice of refusal in time but that is invalid by
reason of its wording, the breach will arise at the moment the notice is given, since
the prohibition on further notices[801A] means that preclusion bites immediately.
Where the bank indicates in its refusal notice that it will return the documents to
the presenter, preclusion will be incurred at the end of the third banking day
following the giving of the notice if the documents have not by then been
despatched by expeditious means of transmission.[801B] Before the instant when
preclusion is incurred, the bank is not in breach; its liability is confined to losses
incurred by the presenter after that instant.[801C]

[801A] Above, para.23–180.
[801B] Above, para.23–183.
[801C] *Fortis Bank SA/NV v Indian Overseas Bank (No.3)* [2011] EWHC 538
(Comm); [2012] 1 All E.R. (Comm) 41 at [31].

18.   RECOURSE

Damages claims in tort

[*fnn.833 and 834, delete "Standard Chartered Bank … 1 A.C. 959" from* **23–262**
fn.834 and add it to fn.833 after "could not be proved);"]

19.   BANKS' SECURITY RIGHTS OVER THE GOODS AND PROCEEDS OF RESALE

Creation of pledge in favour of nominated and issuing banks

[*At the end of the first paragraph, after* "the right of pledge" *insert*] **23–264**
Enforcement of the security right may entail the incurring of liabilities
under the contract of carriage by virtue of s.3 of the Carriage of Goods by Sea
Act 1992. It is, however, inherently implausible that a bank with a security
interest only would undertake potentially significant liabilities under the
contract of carriage unless through s.3 of the 1992 Act as an incident to enforcement of its security. Consequently, it requires compelling evidence to prove an
intention on the part of a bank to engage with the contract of carriage qua principal through the agency of the party that procures the contract and is named as
the shipper.[846A]

[846A] *Fortis Bank SA/NV v Indian Overseas Bank (No.3)* [2011] EWHC 538
(Comm); [2012] 1 All E.R. (Comm) 41 at [66].

20.   THE FLEXIBILITY OF DOCUMENTARY CREDITS

(a)   *Transferable Credits*

No right to a transfer

23–270   [*last line, after* "transfer," *insert new fn.861A*]

861A For advance consent to novation at common law, see *Habibsons Bank Ltd v Standard Chartered Bank (Hong Kong) Ltd* [2010] EWCA Civ 1335; [2011] Q.B. 943 at [21]–[22].

CHAPTER 24

AUTONOMOUS GUARANTEES

1.   INTRODUCTION: ORTHODOX AND AUTONOMOUS GUARANTEES

[*After* "no payment will be claimed under an autonomous guarantee." *insert*]   **24–001**
The commercial line between letters of credit and autonomous guarantees may, however, blur. Compliance problems under the UCP may suggest that a preferable approach to a letter of credit in fulfilment of the primary payment obligation under the underlying contract may be for payment to be made against a more rudimentary trigger in return for an autonomous guarantee enabling recovery of the money under the terms of the guarantee but intended to be triggered in the event of default on the underlying contract. Legally, the two autonomous instruments may respond to different levels of obligation of the underlying contract: a payment credit to the buyer's primary obligation to pay for the goods, a guarantee to the seller's secondary obligation to pay damages for breach of contract.[1A] This, however, is to overlook that, commercially, a payment credit and a payment-plus-guarantee package may respond to the same imperative, namely to keep the life-blood of international trade flowing by facilitating and ensuring payment to the seller while providing reassurance to the buyer that it will not find itself without both performance and money.[1B]
Significant doctrinal differences separate autonomous guarantees from orthodox guarantees. The exposure of an orthodox guarantor to liability co-extensive to that of the principal debtor gives rise to a duty on the part of the creditor to disclose to the putative orthodox guarantor any contract or other dealing between the creditor and the debtor that renders the debt to be secured

[127]

materially different from that which the guarantor might naturally expect. Co-extensive liability imports also that any material variation to the underlying relationship, potentially altering the guarantor's liability, discharges the guarantee. Under an autonomous guarantee, however, the guarantor's liability is not co-extensive with that of the principal debtor but determined entirely by the terms of the guarantee, wholly independently of what may happen in the underlying relationship. In consequence, the disclosure obligation and material variation defence do not apply.[1C] In addition, s.4 of the Statute of Frauds 1677, which imposes the formalities of writing and signature on an orthodox guarantee, is rendered inapplicable by the nature of an autonomous guarantee as giving rise to a primary obligation. Moreover, an autonomous guarantee, being a normal arm's length commercial transaction entered into by the guarantor in return for a fee, falls to be construed in accordance with the normal approach to contractual interpretation and is not subject to the stricter approach to interpretation applicable to orthodox guarantees.[1D]

[1A] This point has been emphasised in Singaporean case law concerned with the circumstances under which an injunction may be granted to prevent payment under an autonomous guarantee: see below, para.24–033.
[1B] The extent to which this is true may depend on the commercial context. It is unclear to what extent parallels can be drawn between international sales of goods and construction contracts, in which latter context the vast majority of reported case law relating to autonomous guarantees has arisen.
[1C] *WS Tankship II BV v Kwangju Bank Ltd* [2011] EWHC 3103 (Comm) at [143]–[144], [149].
[1D] At [127].

Autonomous or secondary guarantee

24–003   [*Line 21, after fn.9 delete* "Fourthly ... underlying contract." *and existing fn.10. Insert*]
    Fourthly, incorporation of a set of uniform rules that articulates a clear principle of independence from the underlying contract is an extremely strong indicator of an autonomous instrument,[10] although the fact that no such rules have been incorporated is an entirely neutral factor of no relevance to the instrument's characterisation.[10A]

[10] *Meritz Fire & Marine Insurance Co Ltd v Jan de Nul NV* [2011] EWCA Civ 827; [2012] 1 All E.R. (Comm) 182 at [19]. Although the instrument may reveal an inconsistency between the autonomy principle as proclaimed in the incorporated rules and the bespoke provisions of the instrument, in which case the interpretation of the instrument as a whole may indicate characterisation as an orthodox guarantee: *Meritz Fire* [2010] EWHC 3362; [2011] 1 C.L.C. 48 at [67]–[70].

[10A] *WS Tankship II BV v Kwangju Bank Ltd* [2011] EWHC 3103 (Comm) at [123].

[Insert after fn.16]

In the light, however, of the potentially dramatic impact of such clauses, they are construed strictly and any ambiguity is resolved in favour of the guarantor (and therefore in favour of characterisation of the instrument as an orthodox guarantee). In particular, courts will enquire closely to see whether the evidence to which the clause speaks is conclusive evidence of the existence of liability (so that the guarantee functions as an autonomous instrument) or merely of the quantum of liability in the event that liability is proved (consistent with the guarantee being orthodox in character).[16A]

[16A] *Vossloh Aktiengesellschaft v Alpha Trains (UK) Ltd* [2010] EWHC 2443 (Ch); [2011] 2 All E.R. (Comm) 307 at [50]–[51].

5. Two Fundamental Principles: Irrevocability and Autonomy

(b) *Autonomy*

Fraud requires dishonesty of the beneficiary

[Line 3, after fn.62 insert]   **24–020**

In the context of a documentary credit, fraud connotes the absence of an honest belief in the genuineness and validity of the documents tendered or in the truthfulness of the statements made in those documents. In the context of an autonomous guarantee, fraud connotes the absence of an honest belief in either the entitlement to claim under the guarantee or in the amount claimed. An honest but mistaken belief in the legitimacy of the claim is not fraud.[62A]

[62A] *AES-3C Maritza East 1 EOOD v Crédit Agricole Corporate and Investment Bank* [2011] EWHC 123 (TCC); [2011] B.L.R. 249 at [48].

[After the new text just inserted, insert paragraph break]

Banks not instructed by the applicant

[fn.106, after "at p.200 (doubtful)." *insert]*   **24–029**

A duty of care was rejected in *Bank of Taiwan v Union Syndicate Corp* [1981] 1 H.K.C. 205 at p.213.

Enjoining a beneficiary from claiming or receiving payment

[Line 12, after "alternative remedy" *insert]*   **24–030**

or of the general balance of convenience

[Line 14, after "last point must be correct," *insert new fn.109A]*

[109A] *Simon Carves Ltd v Ensus UK Ltd* [2011] EWHC 657 (TCC); [2011] B.L.R. 340 at [40]–[42] (noting with respect to the balance of convenience the reputational damage to an applicant that a call on a bond may entail and the adverse impact that a call may have on the applicant's prospects of obtaining additional bond facilities or of qualifying for further tendering competitions).

[*fn.111, after* "[2001] 1 W.L.R. 1800 at [31]" *insert*]
; *Simon Carves Ltd v Ensus UK Ltd* [2011] EWHC 657 (TCC); [2011] B.L.R. 340 at [29], [33(b)]

Unconscionability as the basis for enjoining the beneficiary under an autonomous guarantee

24–033　　[*Para.2, line 14, after* "receipt of money" *insert*]
payable in satisfaction of the applicant's secondary obligation to compensate for a breach of the underlying contract

[*fn.126, line 2, after* "604 at [24]" *insert*]
; *JBE Properties Pte Ltd v Gammon Pte Ltd* [2010] SGCA 46; [2011] 2 S.L.R. 47 at [10]

[*Para.3, line 2, after* "for English law" *insert*]
, in the absence of a fundamental re-assessment by the Supreme Court,

[*Para.3, line 10, after fn.129, delete* "However" *and insert*]
It is, however, unclear whether the English courts would consider a fully-fledged unconscionability exception accompanied by the uncertainty inherent in a fact-sensitive concept reflective of "some notion of fairness"[129A] appropriate in the world of autonomous undertakings on the basis that the entire point of autonomy is that, outwith the inevitable exception of fraud, payment should be made first and any detailed factual enquiries between the parties to the underlying contract should follow second. Moreover,

[129A] See *Shanghai Electric Group Co Ltd v PT Merak Energi Indonesia* [2010] SGHC 2; [2010] 2 S.L.R. 329 *per* Lee Seiu Kin J. at [27], [38]–[39].

[*Insert new para.24–033A*]

Injunctions issued by foreign courts

24–033A　　An English court will not order a contracting party to perform a contract when performance would be illegal according to the law of the place of performance.[130A] Accordingly, where an autonomous guarantee is governed by English law but provides for payment in a foreign jurisdiction and a court of that jurisdiction has granted an injunction prohibiting payment, an English court will not compel the guarantor to pay. It will, nevertheless, grant judgment in the sum of the amount payable under the guarantee, the judgment not to be enforceable while payment remains illegal in the place of performance. It will then be for the foreign court to decide whether to lift the injunction.[130B]

[130A] *Ralli Bros v Cia Naviera Sota y Aznar* [1920] 2 K.B. 287.

^{130B} *AES-3C Maritza East 1 EOOD v Crédit Agricole Corporate and Investment Bank* [2011] EWHC 123 (TCC); [2011] B.L.R. 249 at [67]–[69].

6.   TIME AND PLACE OF PRESENTATION

Extension of time for presentation

[*line 11, after* "would not" *insert*]
have

24–036

7.   REALISATION OF AN AUTONOMOUS GUARANTEE

Time for examination

[*Line 21, after* "unreasonable." *insert paragraph break*]

24–042

[*Add at the end of fn.148*]
The guarantee may, of course, always provide for a different time period: see, for example, *AES-3C Maritza East 1 EOOD v Crédit Agricole Corporate and Investment Bank* [2011] EWHC 123 (TCC); [2011] B.L.R. 249 (displacing the vaguer "reasonable time" formulation of URDG 458 art.10(a) with a period of three banking days following the date of receipt of the demand).

Notice of demand

[*line 18, after* "receipt of a demand." *insert new fn.154A*]

24–045

^{154A} In the case of an "extend or pay" demand (below, para.24–064), notification of the period of suspension under URDG 758 art.23(c) satisfies the art.16 duty to inform.

9.   THE DEMAND FOR PAYMENT

Documentary demand

[*Add new fn.184A at the end of the text*]

24–058

^{184A} At common law, there is no absolute theoretical objection to the terms of an autonomous guarantee rendering it payable on proof of fact, but such an analysis runs counter to the commercial purpose of autonomy and denies the guarantor safety of payment in the absence of a confession of breach by the applicant. Such an analysis, therefore, lacks commercial credibility generating a bias in favour of autonomous guarantees being payable upon a compliant documentary demand: *Esal (Commodities) Ltd v Oriental Credit Ltd* [1985] 2 Lloyd's Rep. 546 at p.549; *IE Contractors Ltd v Lloyds Bank Plc* [1990] 2 Lloyd's Rep. 496 at p.501. Indeed, an instrument that is not so triggered may on analysis prove to be an orthodox rather than an autonomous guarantee.

Demand and statement of default under URDG 758

24–062   [*Add new fn.196A at the end of para.2 after* "as they have been excluded."]

196A See, for example, *AES-3C Maritza East 1 EOOD v Crédit Agricole Corporate and Investment Bank* [2011] EWHC 123 (TCC); [2011] B.L.R. 249 (URDG 458, art.20 excluded).

"Extend or pay" demand

24–064   [*line 6, after* "ordinary demand for payment.' " *insert new fn.201A*]

201A However, a mere request for an extension cannot, of itself, be construed as importing a demand for payment should the request be declined: *British Arab Commercial Bank Plc v Bank of Communications* [2011] EWHC 281 (Comm); [2011] 1 Lloyd's Rep. 664.

10.   Consequences of a Determination of Compliance

Excessive payment

24–068   [*fn.213, at the end after* "C.L.R. 443" *add*]
         ; *Pun Serge v Joy Head Investments Ltd* [2010] SGHC 182; [2010] 4 S.L.R. 478 at [11]–[14].

[*Insert new para.24–068A*]

Inadequate payment

24–068A   The nature of an autonomous guarantee as a security rather than a liquidated damages clause dictates also that, should the amount payable under the instrument prove inadequate to compensate the beneficiary for the loss suffered by the event triggering the call for payment, the beneficiary will be entitled to claim from the applicant damages in a sum equal to the excess loss.215A

215A *Comdel Commodites Ltd v Siporex Trade SA* [1997] 1 Lloyd's Rep. 424 at p.431; *Pun Serge v Joy Head Investments Ltd* [2010] SGHC 182; [2010] 4 S.L.R. 478.

11.   Presentation Considered Non-Complying

[*Insert new para.24–071A*]

A single notice

24–071A   URDG 758 art.24(d) specifies that refusal must be communicated by "a single notice" of refusal to the presenter of the demand. In this, URDG 758 mirrors UCP

600 and reference may be made to the discussion of a single notice in that context.[222A] ISP98, in contrast, contains no such stipulation but focuses rather upon whether notice of dishonour has been given in time.[222B] If indeed no requirement of a single notice of dishonour is implicit in ISP98, a beneficiary that is prejudiced by the omission of a discrepancy from a notice of dishonour (in that an otherwise compliant representation is rejected and the discrepancy, if stated in the original notice of dishonour, could and would have been remedied) may, nevertheless, be able to argue that the issuer is estopped at common law from raising the omitted discrepancy.[222C]

[222A] Above, para.23–180.
[222B] See, for example, ISP98 r.5.02(b)(ii).
[222C] See above, para.23–187.

Time for giving a notice of rejection under URDG 758

[*fn.224, delete* "See also *Fortis . . .* [76]." *and insert*]   **24–072**
Contrast the understanding in the context of UCP 600 art.16 of acting with reasonable promptness (with respect to returning documents pursuant to a notice of refusal), discussed above, para.23–183.

12.   REIMBURSEMENT

Reimbursement rights at common law

[*Insert at the end of the text*]   **24–079**
Clear wording in the counter-guarantee will be required to render the making of a reimbursement claim within a specified period of time of honouring a claim under the autonomous guarantee a condition precedent to the right to reimbursement. Accordingly, a provision that reimbursement would be available provided a claim was made under the guarantee by a specified time and date and the reimbursement claim was made "soonest thereafter" could not be construed as requiring the reimbursement claim to be made immediately or within any particular timeframe. The wording was deliberately imprecise and non-specific.[232A]

[232A] *British Arab Commercial Bank Plc v Bank of Communications* [2011] EWHC 281 (Comm); [2011] 1 Lloyd's Rep. 664 at [67].

Reimbursement rights under URDG 758

[*fnn.239–241. In all three footnotes, delete* "ISP98 r" *and insert*]   **24–082**
URDG 758 art

CHAPTER 25

EXPORT CREDIT GUARANTEES

Note: The ECGD now uses the "operating name": "UK Export Finance".
It has a new website: *www.ukexportfinance.gov.uk*.

1.   INTRODUCTION

Insurance and guarantee providers

25–003   [*Add at the end of the text*]
Indeed, UK Export Finance states explicitly that it will not provide cover unless
it can be demonstrated that cover is unavailable from the private sector.

The ECGD

25–004   [*fn.7, substitute for website reference*]
www.ukexportfinance.gov.uk

Role of the ECGD

25–005   The "Mission Statement" has been redrafted as "Mission and Principles"
(available on UK Export Finance's website), with little change in substance.

2.   EXPORT AND INVESTMENT GUARANTEES ACT 1991

Other provisions

[Add at the end of fn.19]   **25–010**
Section 7(4) was repealed by Statute Law (Repeals) Act 2004, Sch.1(16)(2)
para.1 on July 22, 2004.

5.   OTHER ECGD FACILITIES

New facilities

[Delete existing text apart from first sentence and insert]   **25–045**
However, with the emphasis now on UK Export Finance acting in a comple-
mentary manner to the private sector, those facilities which that sector is able to
provide have been withdrawn. Recently, a number of new schemes have been
made available in conjunction with participating banks. In both the "Bond Support
Scheme" and the "Export Working Capital Scheme", UK Export Finance shares
the risks with banks issuing bonds or making loans (respectively) of not being
reimbursed by the exporter. In the "Foreign Exchange Credit Support Scheme",
UK Export Finance increases its guarantee to the bank in the context of the Export
Working Capital Scheme to cover the bank's provision of hedging protection to
the exporter against foreign exchange rate movements. A scheme of longer
standing is the "Project Financing Scheme" and this will now briefly be
considered.

7.   INTERNATIONAL ASPECTS

EU Harmonising measures

[Add at the end of the text]   **25–053**
These "temporary" measures remain in place: see most recently the
Commission's Communication "Temporary Union framework for State aid measures to support access to finance in the current financial and economic crisis"
(2011/C 6/05).

Part Eight

CONFLICT OF LAWS

CHAPTER 26

CONFLICT OF LAWS

1. Preliminary Considerations

Scope and arrangement of this chapter

26–001   [*Insert before* "The distinct topic"]
See also Fentiman, *International Commercial Litigation* (2010), especially
Pt III. See also (from a Scottish law perspective) Beaumont and McEleavy,
Anton's Private International Law (3rd edn, 2011), especially ch.10 (contract) and
ch.21 (property).

[*Add at the end of fn.2*]
; see also Czepalak (2011) 7 J. Priv. Int. L. 393.

The characterisation of "goods" in conflict of laws

26–004   [*Add at the end of the text*]
The European Commission's Proposal for a Regulation on a Common European
Sales Law (CESL) COM (2011) 635 final (on which, see para.26–220 and
Appendix 1, below), art.2(h) defines goods as "any tangible movable items" but
excludes (i) electricity and natural gas; and (ii) water and other types of gas unless
they are put up for sale in a limited volume or set quantity.

2. Common Law: The Relevance and Role of the Proper Law Doctrine

Absence of express or implied choice

26–008   [*fn.52, insert before* "As to the position under"]
See also *British Arab Commercial Bank Plc v Bank of Communications* [2011]
EWHC 281 (Comm); [2011] 1 Lloyd's Rep. 664, especially at [28].

Examination of all relevant factors

26–009   [*Add at the end of fn.58*]
On the possibility of different laws being applied to different issues at common
law see *Lexington Insurance Co v AGF Insurance Ltd* [2009] UKHL 40; [2010] 1
A.C. 180, especially at [99].

3. The Rome I Regulation and the Rome Convention

(a)   *General Considerations*

26–017   **Purpose of the Convention and the Rome I Regulation**

[*Add at the end of fn.122*]

[138]

The Judgments Regulation is currently undergoing a process of reform: see the European Commission's Proposal of December 14, 2010 COM (2010) 748 final.

Situations to which the Regulation and the Convention apply

[*Add at the end of fn.162*]
The contractual effects of gifts will normally fall within the scope of the Rome Convention (and the Rome I Regulation): see *Gorjat v Gorjat* [2010] EWHC 1537 (Ch) at [10].

26–023

Specific exclusions

[*Add at the end of fn.165*]
On the question whether, and to what extent, the Rome I Regulation may be applicable to arbitrations in EU Member States, see Yüksel, (2011) 7 J. Priv. Int. L.149. See also *Sulamerica Cia Nacional de Seguros SA v Enesa Engenharia SA* [2012] EWCA Civ 638.

26–024

[*Add at the end of the second sentence of fn.169, after* Continental Enterprises *case reference*]
; *Debt Collect London Ltd v SK Slavia Praha-Fotbal AS* [2010] EWHC 57 (QB) at [14]

[*Add at the end of fn.175*]
On the ambit of this exclusion, see Boonk [2011] L.M.C.L.Q. 227.

No *renvoi*

[*Add at the end of fn.202*]
On *renvoi* and arbitration, see *Dallah Real Estate & Tourism Holding Co* [2010] UKSC 46; [2011] 1 A.C. 763 at [124].

26–026

[*Add at the beginning of fn.204*]
See, for example, *Kingspan Environmental Ltd v Borealis A/S* [2012] EWHC 1147 (Comm), where the court considered the application of the governing law, Danish law, including the relevant provisions of the Vienna Sales Convention applicable in Denmark.

[*Add at the end of fn.206*]
Exclusion of the doctrine of *renvoi* prohibits a court from having regard to the choice of law rules of the foreign country whose law is identified by English choice of law rules. It does not, however, prevent an English court from having regard to the intended ambit of a particular foreign rule, including, in particular, whether it is intended to apply in cross-border cases: see *Dallah Real Estate and Tourism Holding Co v Ministry of Religious Affairs, Government of Pakistan* [2010] UKSC 46; [2011] 1 A.C. 763.

(b)   *Choice of Law by the Parties*

Choice of non-state law

26–030   *[Add at the end of fn.237]*
See also Tang (2012) 5 I.J.P.L. 22. See further *Dallah Real Estate & Tourism Holding Co* [2010] UKSC 46, [2011] 1 A.C. 763.

Making the choice of law

26–031   *[Add at the end of fn.250]*
On implied choice of law under the Rome Convention, see further *FR Lurssen Werft GMBH & Co KG v Halle* [2010] EWCA Civ 587; [2011] 1 Lloyd's Rep. 265; *Chunilal v Merrill Lynch International Inc* [2010] EWHC 1467 (Comm); *Gard Marine & Energy Ltd v Tunnicliffe* [2010] EWCA Civ 1052; [2011] I.L.Pr. 10; *Stonebridge Underwriting Ltd v Ontario Municipal Insurance Exchange* [2010] EWHC 2279 (Comm); [2010] 2 C.L.C. 349; *British Arab Commercial Bank Plc v Bank of Communications* [2011] EWHC 281 (Comm); [2011] 1 Lloyd's Rep. 664; *Golden Ocean Group Ltd v Salgaocar Mining Industries Pty Ltd* [2012] EWCA Civ 265. See also (in respect of contracts of guarantee) *Star Reefers Pool Inc v JFC Group Co Ltd* [2012] EWCA Civ 14; *Emeraldian LP v Wellmix Shipping Ltd* [2010] EWHC 1411 (Comm); [2010] 1 C.L.C. 993; *Lawlor v Sandvik Mining & Construction Mobile Crushers & Screens Ltd* [2012] EWHC 1188 (QB).

[Add at the end of fn.253]
On the incorporation of a choice of law clause, see *SSL International Plc v TTK LIG Ltd* [2011] EWCA Civ 1170, where the standard terms of the claimant, including an English choice of law clause, were found not to have been incorporated. See also *Kingspan Environmental Ltd v Borealis A/S* [2012] EWHC 1147 (Comm), in which it was found that the supplier's standard terms of conditions, including a choice of Danish law, had been incorporated into a contract in circumstances where the purchaser did not object to them and did not have terms on its purchase orders.

Subsequent conduct

26–033   *[Add after* FR Lurssen Werft *case reference in fn.271]*
(The decision was affirmed without the need to resolve this issue: see [2010] EWCA Civ 587, [2011] 1 Lloyd's Rep. 265, at [22])

Limitations on choice of law by the parties

26–037   *[Insert before* "See further Hill" *fn.293]*
In *E-Date Advertising GmbH v X* and *Martinez v MGN Ltd* (C-509/09 and C-161/10) [2012] I.L. Pr. 8, the ECJ held that the "country of origin" principle in art.3 of EC Directive 2000/31 ("Directive on electronic commerce") did not create a choice of law rule in favour of the law of the service provider's place of establishment for matters within its scope and so did not affect the application of the Rome I Regulation. It concluded that:

"[A]rt.3 . . . must be interpreted as not requiring transposition in the form of a specific conflict-of-laws rule. Nevertheless, in relation to the coordinated field, Member States must ensure that, subject to the derogations authorised in accordance with the conditions set out in art.3(4) of Directive 2000/31, the provider of an electronic commerce service is not made subject to stricter requirements than those provided for by the substantive law applicable in the Member State in which that service provider is established."

See also *G v Cornelius de Visser* (C-292/10), judgment of March 15, 2012.

Provisions of law that cannot be derogated from by agreement: article 3(3)

[*Add at the end of fn.297*]   26–038
On art.3(3) of the Rome Convention, see *Emeraldian LP v Wellmix Shipping Ltd* [2010] EWHC 1411 (Comm), at [174].

Overriding mandatory provisions of English law

[*Insert before* "For detailed discussion of" *in fn.331*]   26–044
See also *VB Pénzügyi Lízing Zrt v Schneider* C-137/08 [2011] 2 C.M.L.R. 1.
Overriding mandatory provisions of the place of perfomance   26–045

[*Add at the end of fn.343*]
See also Sanchez Lorenzo (2010) 12 Yb. P.I.L. 67.

Public policy

[*Insert before* "For the relationship between" *in fn.361*]   26–046
On art.16 of the Rome Convention, see *BGC Capital Markets (Switzerland) LLC v Rees* [2011] EWHC 2009 (QB).

[*Add at the end of fn.361*]
See also Chong (2012) 128 L.Q.R. 88; Kramberger Skerl (2011) 7 J. Priv. Int. L. 461.

Contracts governed by the Rome Convention—the three conditions of article 5(2)

[*Add at the end of fn.388*]   26–051
See also *Hillside (New Media) Ltd v Baasland* [2010] EWHC 3336 (Comm); [2010] 2 C.L.C. 986 at [42]–[43].

[*Add at the end of fn.419*]   26–055
See further entry at para.26–037, fn.293, above.

[*Add at the end of fn.421*]
See also *Hillside (New Media) Ltd v Baasland* [2010] EWHC 3336 (Comm); [2010] 2 C.L.C. 986 at [42]–[43].

Application to contract concluded "online": the Rome I Regulation

26–058   *[Add at the end of the text]*

In *Pammer v Reederei Karl Schlüter GmbH & Co KG*,[435A] the ECJ considered the application of art.15(1)(c) of the Judgments Regulation to consumer contracts and internet activity. This provision is in the same terms as the pre-conditions in art.6 of the Rome I Regulation. The reference concerned two cases where consumers had purchased services using the internet from companies based in different Member States, after having obtained information about them online. The ECJ ruled that in order to determine whether a business using a website (whether its own or that of an intermediary) can be considered to be "directing" its activity to the consumer's home state, it should be ascertained whether, prior to the conclusion of any contract with the consumer, it is apparent from the website and the trader's overall activity that the trader was envisaging doing business with consumers in one or more Member States, including the consumer's home Member State, in the sense that it was minded to conclude a contract with them.

It went on to provide a non-exhaustive list of potentially relevant indicators that the business was "directing" its activities to the consumer's home state, including: the international nature of the activity; mention of itineraries from other Member States for going to the place where the trader is established; use of a language or a currency other than the language or currency generally used in the Member State in which the trader is established with the possibility of making and confirming the reservation in that other language; mention of telephone numbers with an international code; outlay of expenditure on an internet referencing service in order to facilitate access to the trader's site or that of its intermediary by consumers domiciled in other Member States; use of a top-level domain name other than that of the Member State in which the trader is established; and mention of an international clientele composed of customers domiciled in various Member States. The national court in question should determine whether such evidence exists.

By contrast, the ECJ ruled that the mere accessibility of the trader's or the intermediary's website in the Member State in which the consumer is domiciled is insufficient. The same is true of mention of an email address and of other contact details, or of use of a language or a currency which are generally used in the Member State in which the trader is established.

It is instructive to compare the ECJ's judgment to the joint declaration by the Council and the Commission on art.15(1)(c), which is referred to in Recital (24) of the Rome I Regulation (which Recital confirms that the equivalent provisions in the Judgments Regulation and Rome I Regulation should have the same meaning). The Joint Declaration states that:

"the mere fact that an Internet site is accessible is not sufficient for Article 15 to be applicable, although a factor will be that this Internet site solicits the conclusion of distance contracts and that a contract has actually been concluded at a distance, by whatever means. In this respect, the language or currency which a website uses does not constitute a relevant factor."

Hence, the ECJ's conclusion that the mere accessibility of a website does not trigger the application of the consumer protection rules is consistent with the Joint

Declaration. Its conclusion that the currency and language of the website may be relevant facts is, by contrast, contrary to the Joint Declaration. It can, however, be presumed that the ECJ's approach in *Pammer* will also be followed and applied in the Rome I Regulation context.

Compare, on the application of the Judgments Regulation to torts allegedly committed via the internet, Provisions that cannot be derogated from by agreement *E-Date Advertising GmbH v X* and *Martinez v MGN Ltd*.[435B]

[*Insert before* "See also Office of Fair Trading" *in fn.442*]   **26–060**
See also Consumer Credit (EU Directive) Regulations 2010 SI 2010/1010.

[435A] (C-585/08) [2011] 2 All E.R. (Comm) 888.
[435B] (C-509/09 and C-161/10) [2012] I.L. Pr. 8. See also *Painer v Standard Verlags GmbH* (C-145/10) [2012] E.C.D.R. 6; and *Wintersteiger AG v Products 4U Sondermaschinenbau GmbH* (C-523/10) [2012] E.T.M.R. 31.

(c)   *Applicable Law in Absence of Choice*

Characteristic performance

[*fn.469, insert before* "The same view has been taken in Scotland"]   **26–065**
; *Chalbury McCouat International Ltd v PG Foils Ltd* [2010] EWHC 2050 (TCC); [2011] 1 Lloyd's Rep. 664; *Hillside (New Media) Ltd v Baasland* [2010] EWHC 3336 (Comm), [2010] 2 C.L.C. 986. See also *Cecil v Bayat* [2010] EWHC 641 (Comm) (reversed but not on this point [2011] EWCA Civ 135; [2011] 1 W.L.R. 3086).

[*fn.469, replace final sentence with*]
The characteristic performance of a contract of guarantee is the performance of the guarantor: *Giuliano-Lagarde Report,* pp.20–21; *Emeraldian Ltd Partnership v Wellmix Shipping Ltd* [2010] EWHC 1411 (Comm); [2010] 1 C.L.C. 993; *British Arab Commercial Bank Plc v Bank of Communications* [2011] EWHC 281 (Comm); [2011] 1 Lloyd's Rep. 664; *Golden Ocean Group Ltd v Salgaocar Mining Industries Pvt Ltd* [2011] EWHC 56 (Comm); [2011] 1 C.L.C. 125. The donor of a gift is the characteristic performer: see *Gorjat v Gorjat* [2010] EWHC 1537 (Ch). A party who contractually warrants that he has the requisite authority is the characteristic performer: *Golden Ocean Group Ltd v Salgaocar Mining Industries Pty Ltd* [2012] EWCA Civ 265. On characteristic performance and agency, see also *Lawlor v Sandvik Mining & Construction Mobile Crushers & Screens Ltd* [2012] EWHC 1188 (QB).

(d)   *The Rome I Regulation—Presumptions*

Sale of goods

[*Add new fn.494A after* "It is therefore the case that the law of the place of the   **26–070**
seller's habitual residence will usually be the governing law of a contract of sale of goods."]

For an example of the identification of the governing law of a sale of goods contract in the absence of choice under the Rome I Regulation, see *SSL International Plc v TTK LIG Ltd* [2011] EWCA Civ 1170 at [82].

[*Add at the end of the text*]
In *Electrosteel Europe SA v Edil Centro SpA*,[505A] the ECJ applied its decision in *Car Trim GmbH v Keysafety Systems Srl*[505B] to a sale of goods contract. Article 5(1)(b) of the Judgments Regulation states that, in the case of the sale of goods, the place of performance of an obligation is the place where, "under the contract," the goods were delivered or should have been delivered. The ECJ held that the phrase "under the contract" requires the national court to consider all the relevant provisions of that contract which are capable of clearly identifying that place, including terms and clauses which are generally recognised and applied through the usages of international trade or commerce, such as the Incoterms drawn up by the International Chamber of Commerce in the version published in 2000.

If it is impossible to determine the place of delivery on that basis, without referring to the substantive law applicable to the contract, the place of delivery is the place where the physical transfer of the goods took place, as a result of which the purchaser obtained, or should have obtained, actual power of disposal over those goods at the final destination of the sales transaction.

[505A] (C-87/10) [2011] I.L.Pr. 28.
[505B] (C-381/08) [2010] E.C.R. I-1255.

Displacing the presumptions: the Rome Conventions

26–073 [*Add at the end of fn.524*]
For more recent decisions on the rebuttal of the presumptions pursuant to art.4(5) of the Rome Convention, see *Gard Marine & Energy Ltd v Tunnicliffe* [2010] EWCA Civ 1052; [2011] I.L.Pr.10; *Cecil v Bayat* [2010] EWHC 641 (Comm) (reversed but not on this point [2011] EWCA Civ 135; [2011] 1 W.L.R. 3086); *British Arab Commercial Bank Plc v Bank of Communications* [2011] EWHC 281 (Comm); [2011] 1 Lloyd's Rep. 664; *Naraji v Shelbourne* [2011] EWHC 3298 (QB); *Lawlor v Sandvik Mining & Construction Mobile Crushers & Screens Ltd* [2012] EWHC 1188 (QB).

4.   Contracts Ancillary to Contract of Sale

Contracts for the carriage of goods

26–082 [*Add at the end of fn.578*]
See also *Scrutton on Charterparties and Bills of Lading* (22nd edn, 2011), pp.460–464; Boonk, [2011] L.M.C.L.Q. 227. On bills of lading, see Ulfbeck [2011] L.M.C.L.Q. 293. On bailment, see Aikens [2011] L.M.C.L.Q. 482. See also (in the context of the Judgments Regulation) *AP Moller-Maersk AS v Sonaec Villas Cen Sad Fadoul* [2010] EWHC 355 (Comm); [2011] 1 Lloyd's Rep. 1.

[*Add at the end of fn.594*]

; Baatz, in Thomas (ed.), *The Carriage of Goods by Sea Under the Rotterdam Rules* (2010), Ch.16; Baatz [2011] L.M.C.L.Q. 208; Alvarez-Rubio (2009) 11 Yb. P.I.L. 171. See also Berlingieri [2010] L.M.C.L.Q. 583; Diamond [2008] L.M.C.L.Q. 135, at pp.183–186; [2009] L.M.C.L.Q. 445; Sturley (2008) 14 J.I.M.L. 461.

[*Add at the end of fn.599*]
See also (in the context of the Hague Rules) *Whitesea Shipping & Trading Corp v El Paso Rio Clara Ltda* [2009] EWHC 2552 (Comm); [2010] 1 Lloyd's Rep. 648.

26–083

Contracts of agency

[*fn.604, insert after Dicey, Morris and Collins reference*]
; *Bowstead and Reynolds on Agency* (19th edn, 2010), ch.12.

26–084

[*Add at the end of fn.608*]
On the law applicable to the power of an agent to bind a principal, see *Rimpacific Navigation Inc v Daehan Shipbuilding Co Ltd* [2009] EWHC 2941 (Comm); [2010] 2 Lloyd's Rep. 236; *Standard Chartered Bank v Ceylon Petroleum Corp* [2011] EWHC 1785 (Comm). On the law applicable to whether an agent had ostensible authority, see *Haugesund Kommune v Depfa ACS Bank* [2010] EWCA Civ 579; [2011] 1 All E.R. 190; *Standard Chartered Bank v Ceylon Petroleum Corporation* [2011] EWHC 1785 (Comm) at [448]; *Cecil v Bayat* [2010] EWHC 641 (Comm), (reversed but not on this point [2011] EWCA Civ 135; [2011] 1 W.L.R. 3086). See also (on agents acting for undisclosed principals) *Hillside (New Media) Ltd v Baasland* [2010] EWHC 3336 (Comm) at [40].

[*Add at the end of fn.611*]
See also *Rossetti Marketing Ltd v Diamond Sofa Company Ltd* [2011] EWHC 2482 (QB).

[*Add at the end of fn.614*]
On the law applicable to contracts of agency under the Rome Convention, see also *Lawlor v Sandvik Mining & Construction Mobile Crushers & Screens Ltd* [2012] EWHC 1188 (QB).

Contracts of insurance

[*Add at the end of fn.621*]
On the law applicable to insurance contracts and the relevance of implied choice at common law, see *Wasa International Insurance Co Ltd v Lexington Insurance Co* [2009] UKHL 40; [2010] 1 A.C. 180, at [90].

26–085

[*Add at the end of fn.623*]
On the applicability of the Rome Convention, see also *Faraday Reinsurance Co Ltd v Howden North America Inc* [2011] EWHC 2837 (Comm).

[*Add at the end of fn.624*]
On implied choice of law and reinsurance under the Rome Convention, see *Gard Marine and Energy Ltd v Tunnicliffe* [2010] EWCA Civ 1052; [2011] Bus.

L.R. 839 at [43]–[44]; *Stonebridge Underwriting Ltd v Ontario Municipal Insurance Exchange* [2010] EWHC 2279 (Comm); [2011] Lloyd's Rep. I.R 171.

[Add at the end of fn.625]
On implied choice of law in insurance contracts, see; *Wasa International Insurance Co Ltd v Lexington Insurance Co* [2009] UKHL 40; [2010] 1 A.C. 180; *Faraday Reinsurance Co Ltd v Howden North America Inc* [2011] EWHC 2837 (Comm).

[Add at the end of fn.627]
On the applicable law in the absence of choice in insurance contracts, see *Faraday Reinsurance Co Ltd v Howden North America Inc* [2011] EWHC 2837 (Comm) at [57].

26–086   *[fn.631, add before final sentence beginning "For the history of the implementation"]*
See also Directive 2009/138/EC of the European Parliament and of the Council of November 25, 2009 on the taking-up and pursuit of the business of Insurance and Reinsurance (Solvency II) (recast), [2009] O.J. L335/1. Directives 64/225/EEC, 73/239/EEC, 73/240/EEC, 76/580/EEC, 78/473/EEC, 84/641/EEC, 87/344/EEC, 88/357/EEC, 92/49/EEC, 98/78/EC, 2001/17/EC, 2002/83/EC and 2005/68/EC, as amended, are repealed with effect from November 1, 2012. Member States are required to implement the provisions of the Directive by October 31, 2012. References to the repealed Directives are thereafter to be construed as references to the Solvency II Directive.

[Add at the end of fn.639]
Where the Rome Convention or Rome I Regulation applies, insurance contracts will also be subject to the rules on overriding mandatory provisions and provisions which cannot be derogated from by agreement (on which, see paras 26–038—26–046, above). In this respect, see Third Parties (Rights Against Insurers) Act 2010, s.18, which states that:

"Except as expressly provided, the application of this Act does not depend on whether there is a connection with a part of the United Kingdom; and in particular it does not depend on—

(a) whether or not the liability (or the alleged liability) of the insured to the third party was incurred in, or under the law of, England and Wales, Scotland or Northern Ireland;
(b) the place of residence or domicile of any of the parties;
(c) whether or not the contract of insurance (or a part of it) is governed by the law of England and Wales, Scotland or Northern Ireland;
(d) the place where sums due under the contract of insurance are payable."

Banking contracts

26–087   *[Add at the end of fn.661]*

On the characteristic performance of a banking contract, see *Hathurani v Jassat* [2010] EWHC 2077 (Ch), considering the competing arguments as to who is the characteristic performer without reaching a concluded view.

5. FORMATION AND VALIDITY OF THE CONTRACT OF SALE

Acts required to conclude the contract

[fn.711, add at the end of the first sentence]   26–090
; *Kingspan Environmental Ltd v Borealis A/S* [2012] EWHC 1147 (Comm), especially at [560] and [612]. See also *Midgulf International Ltd v Group Chimique Tunisien* [2010] EWCA Civ 66; [2010] 1 C.L.C. 113; *Tryggingarfelagio Foroyar P/F v CPT Empresas Maritimas SA* [2011] EWHC 589 (Admlty).

Third parties and agency

[fn.734, add at the end of the first sentence]   26–093
See also *Rimpacific Navigation Inc v Daehan Shipbuilding Co Ltd* [2009] EWHC 2941 (Comm); [2010] 2 Lloyd's Rep. 236; *Standard Chartered Bank v Ceylon Petroleum Corp* [2011] EWHC 1785 (Comm); *Haugesund Kommune v Depfa ACS Bank* [2010] EWCA Civ 579; [2011] 1 All E.R. 190; *Standard Chartered Bank v Ceylon Petroleum Corporation* [2011] EWHC 1785 (Comm) at [448]; *Cecil v Bayat* [2010] EWHC 641 (Comm), (reversed but not on this point [2011] EWCA Civ 135; [2011] 1 W.L.R. 3086); *Hillside (New Media) Ltd v Baasland* [2010] EWHC 3336 (Comm) at [40].

Capacity of natural persons

[Add at the end of fn.756]   26–095
See also *Gorjat v Gorjat* [2010] EWHC 1537 (Ch) at [13]–[15].

Corporate capacity

[Add at the end of fn.761]   26–096
See also *Haugesund Kommune v Depfa ACS Bank* [2010] EWCA Civ 579; [2011] 1 C.L.C. 166; *Standard Chartered Bank v Ceylon Petroleum Corp* [2011] EWHC 1785 (Comm).

Formalities

[Add at the end of fn.773]   26–097
See also *Golden Ocean Group Ltd v Salgaocar Mining Industries Pty Ltd* [2012] EWCA Civ 265. The Court of Appeal ruled that the requirement of s.4 of the Statute of Frauds 1677 for a contract of guarantee to be in writing could be satisfied by a sequence of negotiating emails or other documents whose use was common place in ship chartering and ship sales.

Effect of statutes

26–101   [*Add at the end of fn.808*]
On the international ambit of the Consumer Credit Act 1974, see Bisping
(2012) 8 J. Priv. Int. L. 35.

Unfair Contract Terms Act

26–102   [*Add at the end of fn.816*]
See also Burbidge (2012) 23 I.C.C.L.R. 105.

26–105   [*Add at the end of the text*]
In *Air Transworld Ltd v Bombardier Inc* [2012] EWHC 243 (Comm); [2012] 1
Lloyd's Rep. 349, the claimant was a Gibraltar company controlled by an individual resident in Angola, M. It sought a declaration that it had validly rejected a
private jet aircraft purchased from the defendant Canadian manufacturer. The
aircraft was to be M's private jet and the claimant became the purchaser under the
aircraft purchase agreement by virtue of an assignment agreement. The terms of
the purchase agreement were negotiated at meetings in England and in Portugal.
The purchase agreement was then faxed to Canada for execution by the defendant.
It provided that the warranty obligations and liabilities of the seller and the rights
and remedies of the buyer in the agreement were in lieu of any obligations, representations or liabilities arising by law and the buyer released any such rights. The
purchase agreement was stated to be governed by "the internal laws of England
and Wales, excluding any conflicts of law provisions." More than a year after
delivery, the claimant rejected the aircraft and alleged that it did not correspond
with description, was not of satisfactory quality and was unfit for purpose within
the conditions implied under ss.13 and 14 of the Sale of Goods Act 1979. The
claimant argued that ss.13 and 14 of the Sale of Goods Act 1979 were not excluded.
The defendant relied upon the terms of the purchase agreement excluding liability
arising by statute and claimed that it was not in breach of the warranties set out in
the contract. The defendant further argued that the purchase agreement was an
international supply contract within the meaning of s.26 of the Unfair Contract
Terms Act 1977 and so the exclusion clause was not subject to the test of
reasonableness.
  The court held that the purchase agreement and an assignment agreement were
"international supply contracts" for the purposes of s.26 of the Unfair Contract
Terms Act 1977. It ruled that the reference in s.26(4)(b) of the Unfair Contract
Terms Act 1977 to "the acts constituting the offer and acceptance" meant all of the
relevant acts constituting the offer and acceptance, including the making and
receipt of the offer. It held that s.26(4)(b) was intended to exclude cases where
there was any international element to the formation of the contract, so that the
Act could only apply if all elements of the offer and acceptance occurred in the
same state. It considered that the assignment agreement was the relevant agreement for these purposes. It further noted that at the time of the conclusion of the
purchase agreement and the assignment agreement, it was contemplated that "the
goods in question . . . will be carried, from the territory of one State to the territory
of another" within the meaning of s.26(4)(a), as delivery was to take place in
Canada and the aircraft was to be exported immediately and registered abroad.

The court considered that the choice of law clause did not exclude the application of s.27 of the Unfair Contract Terms Act 1977 since:

"Section 27 does not lay down a unilateral or multilateral conflict of law rule, but merely sets the limits of the application of particular sections of the Act in the circumstances referred to. To disregard section 27 would result in a distorted application of substantive English law, since the statute provides that, in the given circumstances, instead of applying the full gamut of provisions in UCTA, the provisions of section 27, (including the provisions restricting the avoidance of liability arising in contract and in the sale of goods and hire purchase) are not to apply." (at [98]).

It also considered, however, that English law was the governing law of the purchase agreement and assignment agreement solely as a result of the choice of law clause, and thus the test of reasonableness under the 1977 Act did not apply, in accordance with s.27(1) (considered at para.26–103, below).

Choice of law by the parties: a foreign law

[Insert before penultimate paragraph]   **26–111**
In *Kingspan Environmental Ltd v Borealis A/S* [2012] EWHC 1147 (Comm), the supplier of goods had a UK subsidiary company but invoices were stated to be from its Danish parent company. Its standard terms excluded all conditions and warranties as to the quality or fitness for any purpose of the goods. These terms were stated to be governed by the law of the country where Borealis was domiciled. The court held that the question whether these terms were incorporated was a matter for the putative applicable law, namely Danish law. The court found that there was no evidence, for the purposes of s.27 of the Unfair Contract Terms Act 1977, that the choice of Danish law had been made with the intention to evade the relevant provisions of the Act. The contracts were also held to be international sales contracts for the purposes of s.26 of the Act.

Legality

[Add at the end of fn.974]   **26–132**
; *Lilly Icos LLC v 8 PM Chemists Ltd* [2009] EWHC 1905 (Ch); [2010] F.S.R. 95 at [261]–[266].

6.   PROPERTY

(a)   *General Issues*

The *lex situs* principle

[Add at the end of fn.1017]   **26–134**
In *Joint Administrators of Rangers Football Club Plc* [2012] CSOH 55 (Outer House, Court of Session), 2012 S.L.T. 599, the court considered the scope of the Rome Convention and ruled (at [28]) that:

"Article 1(1) states that the rules apply 'to contractual obligations in any situation involving a choice between the laws of different countries.' The creation of an equitable interest intermediate between a personal right and a right *in rem* is to my mind not a contractual obligation which the Convention covers. The Guiliano–Lagarde report on the Rome Convention (O.J. C 282, 31 October 1980) supports this view, stating in its discussion of Article 1 of the Convention: 'Since the Convention is concerned only with the law applicable to contractual obligations, property rights are not covered by these provisions.'"

[*fn.1013, insert after* Oxonica Energy Ltd *case reference*]
; *Blue Sky One Ltd v Mahan Air* [2010] EWHC 631 (Comm), at [154] (noted Forsyth (2010) 6 J. Priv. Int. L. 637; Knight [2010] Conv. 331).

[*Add at the end of fn.1013*]
On the *situs* of choses in action, see *Hillside (New Media) Ltd v Baasland* [2010] EWHC 3336 (Comm); [2010] 2 C.L.C. 986 at [33].

Renvoi

26–135   [*Insert before the last sentence*]
In *Blue Sky One Ltd v Mahan Air,*[1023A] the court rejected the application of the doctrine of *renvoi* in respect of the creation or transfer of *inter vivos* proprietary interests in aircraft.

[1023A] [2010] EWHC 631 (Comm).

[*Add at the end of fn.1025*]
By contrast, the doctrine of *renvoi* still applies to transfers of movable property on death: see *Haji-Ioannou v Frangos* [2009] EWHC 2310 (QB); [2010] 1 All E.R. (Comm) 303.

(c)   *The Passing of Title: The General Rules*

(i)   *Goods not in Transit: No Documents Issued*

The seller as owner

26–143   [*Insert new fn.1064A at the end of the text*]
[1064A]In *Blue Sky One Ltd v Mahan Air* [2010] EWHC 631 (Comm) (noted Forsyth (2010) 6 J. Priv. Int. L. 637; Knight [2010] Conv. 331), the court ruled that the validity of a mortgage of aircraft was governed by the law of its physical *situs* and not by the law of the place of registration of the aircraft (save where the aircraft was in flight over the high seas or a *territorium nullius*). The court went on to reject the application of the doctrine of *renvoi* in respect of aircraft. See also *Wilmington Trust Co v Rolls Royce Plc* [2011] CSOH 151; 2011 G.W.D. 32-681, *Court* of Session (Outer House).

Impact of the law applicable to the contract

26–146   [*Add at the end of fn.1086*]

On the distinction between the contractual and proprietary aspects of sale of goods (and confirming the application of the *lex situs* to the latter), see *Dornoch Ltd v Westminster International BV* [2009] EWHC 1782 (Admlty), at [5]. See also *Blue Sky One Ltd v Mahan Air* [2010] EWHC 631 (Comm). *Cf. Luxe Holding Ltd v Midland Resources Holding Ltd* [2010] EWHC 1908 (Ch); *Perry v Serious Organised Crime Agency* [2011] EWCA Civ 578.

(d)   *Retention of Title*

Claims by original seller against sub-purchaser

[Add at the end of fn.1152] **26–161**
On identifying the governing law under the Private International Law (Miscellaneous Provisions) Act 1995, Part III (prior to the entry into force of the Rome II Regulation) see *VTB Capital Inc v Nutritek International Corp* [2011] EWHC 3107 (Ch); *Kingspan Environmental Ltd v Borealis A/S* [2012] EWHC 1147 (Comm). See also *Fiona Trust & Holding Corp v Privalov* [2010] EWHC 3199 (Comm); *Alliance Bank JSC v Aquanta Corporation* [2011] EWHC 3281 (Comm) ; [2012] 1 Lloyd's Rep. 181.

[Add at the end of fn.1153]
In *Homawoo v GMF Assurances* (C-412/10) [2012] I.L.Pr. 2, the ECJ ruled that national courts were to apply the Rome II Regulation only to events giving rise to damage occurring on or after January 11, 2009. The date on which the proceedings seeking compensation for the damage were brought and the date on which the applicable law was determined by the court seised were irrelevant.

[Add at the end of fn.1154] **26–162**
On the identification of the governing law under the Rome II Regulation, see *Homawoo v GMF Assurances (*C-412/10) [2012] I.L.Pr. 2; *Alliance Bank JSC v Aquanta Corporation* [2011] EWHC 3281 (Comm); [2012] 1 Lloyd's Rep. 181; *VTB Capital Inc v Nutritek International Corp* [2011] EWHC 3107 (Ch). See also *Force India Formula One Team Limited v Malaysia Racing Team Sdn Bhd* [2012] EWHC 616 (Ch); *Innovia Films Ltd v Frito-Lay North America Inc* [2012] EWHC 790 (Pat).

[Add at the end of fn.1165]
See also *Maple Leaf Macro Volatility Master Fund v Rouvroy* [2009] EWHC 257 (Comm). On assignment and voluntary dispositions, see *Gorjat v Gorjat* [2010] EWHC 1537 (Ch) at [10].

[Add at the end of fn.1167]
; Hartley (2011) 60 I.C.L.Q. 29; Møllmann [2011] L.M.C.L.Q. 262.

[Add at the end of fn.1171]
Pursuant to art.27(1) of the Rome I Regulation, the European Commission was to submit a report on the effects of assignment and subrogation on third parties. It commissioned the British Institute of International and Comparative Law to produce this study, entitled a "Study on the Question of Effectiveness of an

Assignment or Subrogation of a Claim Against Third Parties and the Priority of the Assigned or Subrogated Claim over a Right of Another Person." It is available at *http://ec.europa.eu/justice/civil/files/report_assignment_en.pdf.* (set out at 26–086, fn.639, above). On subrogation, see also Third Parties (Rights Against Insurers) Act 2010 s.18 (set out at 26-086, fn.639, above).

Council Regulation on insolvency proceedings

26–164   *[Add at the end of fn.1185]*
On the application of the *lex situs* in the context of the Regulation, see *Polymer Vision R&D Ltd v Van Dooren* [2011] EWHC 2951 (Comm); [2012] I.L.Pr. 14, at [41].

Directive on combating late payment in commercial transactions

26–166   *[Add at the end of the text]*
Directive 2000/35 on combating late payment in commercial transactions will be repealed with effect from March 16, 2013. Member States are required to implement rules to give effect to Directive 2011/7/EU of the European Parliament and of the Council on combating late payment in commercial transactions. Article 9(1) of Directive 2011/7/EU is, however, substantively the same as art.4(1) of Directive 2000/35/EC.

8.   PERFORMANCE OF THE CONTRACT OF SALE

General principles

26–169   *[Add at the end of fn.1208]*
; see also *Wilmington Trust Co v Rolls Royce Plc* [2011] CSOH 151; 2011 G.W.D. 32-681, Court of Session (Outer House).

    [Add at the end of fn.1209]
On the meaning and scope of art.10(1)(b) of the Rome Convention (and the "obscure" nature of the provision) see *Joint Administrators of Rangers Football Club Plc* [2012] CSOH 55 (Outer House, Court of Session); 2012 S.L.T. 599, at [28].

9.   DISCHARGE OF OBLIGATIONS UNDER A CONTRACT OF SALE

General principles

26–186   *[Add at the end of fn.1355]*
See also *Kingspan Environmental Ltd v Borealis A/S* [2012] EWHC 1147 (Comm) at [612].

10.   REMEDIES OF THE SELLER

(b)   *Personal Remedies of the Seller*

Specific aspects of the remedies available

[*Add before the final sentence of fn.1433*]   26–204
See also *Abdel Hadi Abdallah Al Qahtani & Sons Beverage Industry Co v Antliff* [2010] EWHC 1735 (Comm). See also *Commission v Trendsoft* (C-127/03), judgment of July 8, 2004; and *Commission v Huhtamaki Dourdan SA* (C-315/03), judgment of May 12, 2005. See further Bariatti, *Cases and Materials on EU Private International Law* (2011), p.599.

[*Add at the end of fn.1450*]   26–205
On exchange losses caused by late payment and depreciation occurring in the meantime, see also *Milan Nigeria Ltd v Angeliki B Maritime Co* [2011] EWHC 892 (Comm).

Currency questions   26–206

[*Add before the penultimate sentence of fn.1455*]
See also *Karafarin Bank v Dara (No. 2)* [2009] EWHC 3265 (Comm); [2010] 1 Lloyd's Rep. 236; *Addax Bank BSC v Wellesley Partners LLP* [2010] EWHC 1904 (QB); *Milan Nigeria Ltd v Angeliki B Maritime Co* [2011] EWHC 892 (Comm); *Fearns v Anglo-Dutch Paint & Chemical Co Ltd* [2010] EWHC 2366 (Ch); [2011] 1 W.L.R. 366.

[*Add at the end of fn.1456*]
On the currency of account, see *Addax Bank BSC v Wellesley Partners LLP* [2010] EWHC 1904 (QB).

Currency of judgment   26–207

[*Add before the final sentence of fn.1466*]
; see also *Fearns v Anglo-Dutch Paint & Chemical Co Ltd* [2010] EWHC 2366 (Ch); [2011] 1 W.L.R. 366.

12.   PROCEDURE

Procedure governed by the *lex fori*

[*Add at the end of fn.1511*]   26–216
; Garnett, *Substance and Procedure in Private International Law* (2012). See also *Fiona Trust & Holding Corp v Privalov* [2010] EWHC 3199 (Comm).

Limitation of actions

[*Add at the end of fn.1518*]   26–217

Section 2(2) of the Foreign Limitation Periods Act 1984 states that the application of a foreign limitation period shall be contrary to English public policy "to the extent that its application would cause undue hardship to a person who is, or might be made, a party to the action or proceedings." On the meaning of "undue hardship", see *Harley v Smith* [2010] EWCA Civ 78; [2010] C.P. Rep. 33. See also s.1A of the Foreign Limitation Periods Act 1984 on the extension of limitation periods because of mediation of certain cross-border disputes, inserted by SI 2011/1133, Pt 3, reg.29.

[Add at the end of the text]
The Rome I and II Regulations both contain provisions on the law applicable to limitation periods. Sections 1, 2 and 4 of the Foreign Limitation Periods Act 1984 are disapplied where the Rome I or Rome II Regulation applies.

[1521A] See Foreign Limitation Periods Act 1984, s.8; SI 2008/2986; SI 2009/3064.

This includes cases involving conflicts solely between the laws of different parts of the United Kingdom or between one or more parts of the United Kingdom and Gibraltar.

Burden of proof and presumptions

26–218   *[Add at the end of fn.1523]*
See also *Fiona Trust & Holding Corp v Privalov* [2010] EWHC 3199 (Comm), especially at [94].

[Add at the end of fn.1528]
See also *Fiona Trust & Holding Corp v Privalov* [2010] EWHC 3199 (Comm), especially at [98].

[Insert new para.26–220]

Future Developments: the Proposed Common European Sales Law and choice of law rules

26–220   The European Commission has published a Proposal for a Regulation on a Common European Sales Law (CESL) (COM (2011) 635; see also the Communication from Commission to the European Parliament, the Council, the European Economic and Social Committee and the Committee of the Regions Com (2011) 636 Final). The proposed instrument would apply, at the parties' election, to cross-border contracts of sales of goods and digital content where at least one party is established in an EU Member State. It contains rules on business-to-business and business-to-consumer transactions. The UK Ministry of Justice published a checklist for analysis of the proposal on February 27, 2012 and a Call for Evidence about the impact, possible costs and benefits of CESL, with a view to developing its future position on the proposed Regulation (see *https://consult. justice.gov.uk/digital-communications/common-european-sales-law*). The principal features of CESL are set out in Appendix 1, this Supplement.
CESL would, in effect, amount to a further set of substantive law rules within each Member State. This means that it would not be the applicable law of a contract

for matters within its ambit; rather, it would apply where the governing law is that of a Member State and the matter in question is within the scope of CESL.

The Proposal notes (at p.2 of the Explanatory Memorandum) that the adoption of an optional, harmonised system of law would reduce disparities arising from the potential need to apply the laws of a plethora of States pursuant to the rules on consumer contracts in art.6 of the Rome I Regulation (on which, see paras 26–047 *et seq.*). It states that:

"In cross-border transactions between a business and a consumer, contract law related transaction costs and legal obstacles stemming from differences between different national mandatory consumer protection rules have a significant impact. Pursuant to Article 6 of Regulation 593/2008 of the European Parliament and of the Council of 17 June 2008 on the law applicable to contractual obligations (Rome I), whenever a business directs its activities to consumers in another Member State, it has to comply with the contract law of that Member State. In cases where another applicable law has been chosen by the parties and where the mandatory consumer protection provisions of the Member State of the consumer provide a higher level of protection, these mandatory rules of the consumer's law need to be respected. Traders therefore need to find out in advance whether the law of the Member State of the consumer's habitual residence provides a higher level of protection and ensure that their contract is in compliance with its requirements. The existing harmonisation of consumer law at Union level has led to a certain approximation in some areas but the differences between Member States' laws remain substantial. In e-commerce transactions, traders incur further contract law related costs which stem from the need to adapt the business's website to the legal requirements of each Member State where they direct their activity."

In business-to-business contracts, this factor would appear to be largely irrelevant given the autonomy of the parties to choose the governing law. Nonetheless, the Explanatory Memorandum argues (at p.3) that:

"In cross-border transactions between traders, parties are not subject to the same restrictions on the applicable law. However, the economic impact of negotiating and applying a foreign law is also high. The costs resulting from dealings with various national laws are burdensome particularly for SME [*i.e.* small and medium-sized enterprises.] In their relations with larger companies, SME generally have to agree to apply the law of their business partner and bear the costs of finding out about the content of the foreign law applicable to the contract and of complying with it. In contracts between SME, the need to negotiate the applicable law is a significant obstacle to cross-border trade. For both types of contracts (business-to-business and business-to-consumer) for SME, these additional transaction costs may even be disproportionate to the value of the transaction.

These additional transaction costs grow proportionately to the number of Member States into which a trader exports. Indeed, the more countries they export to, the greater the importance traders attach to differences in contract law as a barrier to trade. SME are particularly disadvantaged: the smaller a company's turnover, the greater the share of transaction costs.

Traders are also exposed to increased legal complexity in cross-border trade, compared to domestic trade, as they often have to deal with multiple national contract laws with differing characteristics.

Dealing with foreign laws adds complexity to cross-border transactions. Traders ranked the difficulty in finding out the provisions of a foreign contract law first among the obstacles to business-to-consumer transactions and third for business-to-business transactions. Legal complexity is higher when trading with a country whose legal system is fundamentally different while it has been demonstrated empirically that bilateral trade between countries which have a legal system based on a common origin is much higher than trade between two countries without this commonality."

CESL is intended to complement the application of the Rome I Regulation and not to provide an alternative to it. Recital (10) of CESL provides that:

"The agreement to use the Common European Sales Law should be a choice exercised within the scope of the respective national law which is applicable pursuant to Regulation (EC) No 593/2008 or, in relation to pre-contractual information duties, pursuant to Regulation (EC) No 864/2007 of the European Parliament and of the Council of 11 July 2007 on the law applicable to non-contractual obligations (Regulation (EC) No 864/2007), or any other relevant conflict of law rule. The agreement to use the Common European Sales Law should therefore not amount to, and not be confused with, a choice of the applicable law within the meaning of the conflict-of-law rules and should be without prejudice to them. This Regulation will therefore not affect any of the existing conflict of law rules."

The way that Rome I and CESL will interrelate is further explained on p.6 of the Explanatory Memorandum:

"The Common European Sales Law will be a second contract law regime within the national law of each Member State. Where the parties have agreed to use the Common European Sales Law, its rules will be the only national rules applicable for matters falling within its scope. Where a matter falls within the scope of the Common European Sales Law, there is thus no scope for the application of any other national rules. This agreement to use the Common European Sales Law is a choice between two different sets of sales law within the same national law and does therefore not amount to, and must not be confused with, the previous choice of the applicable law within the meaning of private international law rules."

Hence, art.11 of the Proposal provides that:

"Where the parties have validly agreed to use the Common European Sales Law for a contract [in accordance with the requirements of art.8 of CESL], only the Common European Sales Law shall govern the matters addressed in its rules. Provided that the contract was actually concluded, the Common European Sales Law shall also govern the compliance with and remedies for failure to comply with the pre-contractual information duties."

In the case of consumer contracts, Recital (12) indicates that:

"Since the Common European Sales Law contains a complete set of fully harmonised mandatory consumer protection rules, there will be no disparities between the laws of the Member States in this area, where the parties have chosen to use the Common European Sales Law. Consequently, Article 6(2) Regulation (EC) No 593/2008, which is predicated on the existence of differing levels of consumer protection in the Member States, has no practical importance for the issues covered by the Common European Sales Law."

Recitals (27) and (28) make it clear (for the avoidance of any doubt) that the applicable law, as identified by the Rome I and II Regulations and other relevant rules of private international law continue to apply to matters outside the ambit of CESL.

It is less clear what should happen if the governing law of the contract is that of a non-Member State. Logic might suggest that if the governing law is that of a non-Member State, then CESL may not be applied. Recital (14), however, states that:

"The use of the Common European Sales Law should not be limited to cross-border situations involving only Member States, but should also be available to facilitate trade between Member States and third countries. Where consumers from third countries are involved, the agreement to use the Common European Sales Law, which would imply the choice of a foreign law for them, should be subject to the applicable conflict-of-law rules"

Since CESL will not be part of the law of a non-Member State, it is not entirely clear what this means, especially as parties are *not* allowed to choose anything other than the law of a recognised legal system and may not directly choose non-state law to govern their contract under the Rome I Regulation (see para.26–030). In some situations, it may be possible to infer a choice of the law of a state in which CESL applies, as where one party is resident in an EU Member State and the other is not. In other cases, however, the search for an implied choice of law may prove elusive. Alternatively, it may be that the parties will incorporate some or all of the provisions of CESL by reference, as permitted by the Rome I Regulation (see para.26–028); but again, such an analysis will not work if the parties instead purport to make a direct choice of CESL to govern their contract.

Nor is it clear what should happen if the parties choose CESL to govern their contract in circumstances where the consumer contract rules of the Rome I Regulation are applicable and the consumer is resident in a non-Member State and seeks to rely on the supplementary protection of the laws of that state which cannot be derogated from by agreement. In such a scenario, either the application of art.6(2) of the Rome I Regulation is precluded, so that the consumer cannot rely on his home law in accordance with art.6(2) of the Rome I Regulation, (contrary to the assertion in Recital (10) of CESL that the operation of the Rome I Regulation will be unaffected) or the consumer may still rely on art.6(2) of the Rome I Regulation (in which case, the assertion in Recital (12) of CESL that art.6(2) of the Rome I Regulation would have no practical significance for issues within the ambit of CESL would not be correct).

[157]

[Insert before existing Appendix renaming existing Appendix as Appendix 2]

APPENDIX 1

A1–001   On October 11, 2011, the European Commission issued a Proposal for a Regulation of the European Parliament and of the Council on a Common European Sales Law (COM (2011) 635 final) (2011/0284 (COD)). The constitutional basis of this initiative is stated to be art.114 (3) of the Treaty on the Functioning of the European Union. Furthermore, in accordance with the subsidiarity principle expressed in art.5 of the Treaty on European Union, the Commission states that problems arising in cross-border transactions are not susceptible to being addressed by national laws (p.10). The Commission's proposal stems from a perception that differences in national contract laws hinder consumers and small-to-medium enterprises (SMEs) from engaging in cross-border trading activity. Without citing evidence, the Commission claims that differences in national contract laws account for trade forgone between Member States in the order of tens of billions of Euros annually (p.3).In making this assessment, the Commission does not distinguish between trade that is lost and trade that is redirected within national borders. The reported response from traders, nevertheless, suggests that national legal difference is a barrier to cross-border trade, especially for consumer sales.

With the aim of improving the workings of the single market, the Commission's proposal is that there be introduced "a self-standing set of contract rules" that would constitute "a second contract law regime within the national law of each Member State" (p.4). The contents of this new contract law are set out in an Annex to the Regulation. The new law would be an optional one (art.3), and so would require the consent of both parties. In its application to consumer sales, the law would dispense with the need for a trader to elicit national consumer protection provisions of a mandatory character, for it would contain "fully harmonised consumer protection rules providing for a high standard of protection" (p.4) (but see entry at para.26–220, above, where the private international law aspects of the Regulation are considered further). In addition, the new law "may be used" in a business to business transaction "if at least one of [the] parties is a small or medium-sized enterprise ('SME')" (Art 7(1)). The new law would therefore be unavailable for other business to business transactions. If, nevertheless, it were voluntarily incorporated by the parties in such contracts, it would not have the status of national law for the purpose of the Rome I Regulation on the law applicable to contractual obligations (reg.593/2008) (discussed in Ch.26). When the new law is adopted, it and it alone is to govern in respect of matters addressed in its rules (art.11). This, oddly, is despite the fact that, subject to exceptions, contracting parties are free to exclude provisions of the new contract law and to derogate from or vary the effect of those provisions (art.1(2)). Furthermore, the choice of the new law implies the exclusion of the Vienna Convention on the International Sale of Goods (recital (25)), though this of course is a matter for the Vienna Convention itself (in its art.6) and not for the Regulation. There are, nevertheless, very clear signs of the great influence exerted by the Vienna Convention on the contents of the new contract law.

If the elimination of national legal difference as a barrier to cross-border trade is the basis of the Commission's proposal, it is not immediately understandable why the proposed new law could not be adopted in all business contracts: the definition of an SME is a somewhat arbitrary matter and the evidence about trading inhibition, such as it may be, is unlikely to support the taking of a sharp distinction between SMEs and other traders. An examination of the proposed law, it should be noted, reveals a substantial number of mandatory, protective provisions that treat SMEs as a type of quasi-consumer. Such provisions are different and less extensive in scope than those that would apply in consumer transactions.

In addition to sale of goods transactions, the new law would be available for related service contracts, as well as for contracts concerning the supply of digital content and service contracts related thereto (art.5). The provisions of the new law concerning consumer contracts incorporate much of the *acquis communautaire* in the area. So far as it would apply to commercial sale of goods contracts, it would deal with a number of general contractual issues that do not arise under the Vienna Convention. For example, the new contract law has provisions dealing with pre-contractual disclosure (Annex arts 23–24) and with vitiating factors, such as mistake (Annex art.48). Unlike the Vienna Convention, it imposes directly on the contracting parties a duty of good faith and fair dealing, which may not be excluded by the contract (Annex art.2). The new law also contains a provision dealing with limitation periods (Annex art.179) and provisions on interest, including one that imposes on traders late in paying the price a swingeing rate of interest at eight percentage points above the central bank rate (Annex art.168(5)(b)).